IMPLEMENTING GLOBAL PERFORMANCE MEASUREMENT SYSTEMS

IMPLEMENTING GLOBAL PERFORMANCE MEASUREMENT SYSTEMS

A Cookbook Approach

Ferdinand Tesoro
Jack Tootson

Jossey-Bass
Pfeiffer
San Francisco

Copyright © 2000 by Jossey-Bass/Pfeiffer
ISBN: 0-7879-4744-X

Library of Congress Cataloging-in-Publication Data

Tesoro, Ferdinand, date.
  Implementing global performance measurement systems : a cookbook approach /
Ferdinand Tesoro, Jack Tootson.
    p.   cm.
  Includes bibliographical references (p.) and index.
  ISBN 0-7879-4744-X (hard : perm. paper)
  1. Organizational effectiveness—Measurement. 2. Performance—Measurement.
I. Tootson, Jack, date. II. Title.
HD58.9 .T47 2000
658.4'013—dc21

99-6786

Printed in the United States of America.

Published by

350 Sansome Street, 5th Floor
San Francisco, California 94104-1342
(415) 433-1740; Fax (415) 433-0499
(800) 274-4434; Fax (800) 569-0443

Visit our website at: www.pfeiffer.com

Acquiring Editor: Matthew Holt
Director of Development: Kathleen Dolan Davies
Copyeditor: Rebecca Taff
Developmental Editor: Maryanne Koschier
Production Manager: Lasell Whipple

Manufacturing Supervisor: Becky Carreño
Interior Design: Paula Goldstein
Jacket Design: Tom Morgan / Blue Design
Illustrations: Lotus Art

Printing 10 9 8 7 6 5 4 3 2 1

To Ferdinand's wife, Theresa, and children, Ryne and Rachel

To Jack's wife, Pam

CONTENTS

PREFACE

When you hear the words performance measurement, what usually comes to mind? Complicated metrics? Pie-in-the-sky targets? Bothersome standards? Time-consuming evaluations? Boring statistics? Probably all of these, and more. The general perception is that it is difficult to design and implement a performance measurement system, and even when it is used in an organization, the system is seldom used effectively to help the company meet its strategic business objectives or manage its resources and people.

Your staff also may have been burned by previous performance measurement efforts and, if asked to participate in another one, may be very resistant: "Oh, no! Here we go again; another exercise in futility." Or they may actually be afraid that such a system will be used against them, in an effort to weed out the marginal performers.

As a performance consultant, human resource development (HRD) professional, or a manager of a business or organization, what can you do? On the one hand, you experience the increased focus on market share, profitability, shareholder confidence, managerial accountability, tactical agility, technology leveraging, and strategic planning in organizations today, so you know that performance measurement is needed more than ever. Your business success depends on it. And yet, you know there may be resistance from your staff to implementing a performance measurement system, and you might even feel a lack of confidence in your own knowledge and skill in designing and implementing such a system—let alone making sure that it is used effectively in your organization.

You are not alone!

In our experience as performance technology consultants, we have met many competent and experienced professionals just like you. They are professionals who see the value in performance measurement and yet are just coming up the learning curve on how to develop and use it in their departments or with the client groups they are supporting. They begin to talk to people or review some of the books on the topic and then become discouraged at the seemingly very technical nature of the task ahead.

Because user-friendly books are in short supply in the field of performance measurement, we wanted to write a book that explains the process of designing and implementing such a system in simple, easy-to-understand and easy-to-use terms. That is the purpose of *Implementing Global Performance Measurement Systems*—to make performance measurement accessible to you so that you can measure progress and ongoing performance and so that you can link this measurement to critical success factors of your business.

For example, if one of your business goals or a client's business goal is to increase market share by 15 percent, this book will show you how to assess whether that is a realistic goal for you and your staff. It will help you determine the capacity and adaptability of your company to support your new goal, the availability of internal and external resources, the current market demand of your product or service, the technological trends that will impact your efforts, and the strategies of your competitors.

Even if your goal is a nebulous one—say, for example, you are a manager in a nonprofit organization and you want to improve the community's perception of the work you have done—we will illustrate how you can evaluate the success of the tactics you use to achieve your goal of enhancing your image in the community. Better yet, we will show you how to package and present your results to your key community leaders.

Intended Audience

As we mentioned before, this book is for managers, HRD professionals, and performance consultants interested in learning more about the field of performance measurement and in increasing their skills in designing and implementing such a system in their organizations. The term *performance consultant* is meant to include all "jobs" that are associated with improving individual and organizational performance, such as the following (Robinson & Robinson, 1995, p. xi):

- Trainer (technical trainer, sales trainer, management development trainer, and so on)
- Training specialist
- Training coordinator
- Training consultant
- Instructional designer
- Instructional systems designer
- Web-based training developer
- Internal or external consultant
- Career developer
- Organization developer
- Media specialist

The tools and techniques presented are applicable to organizations of all sizes and types—even small service-oriented companies, government entities, and private, nonprofit organizations. The only essential criterion for any company or organization is the desire to succeed in its mission.

For ease of readability, we will address the reader as a performance consultant, understanding that the tasks of design and implementation for a performance measurement system remain the same for anyone who is "consulting" on how to improve performance in the organization.

September 1999   Ferdinand Tesoro
Round Rock, Texas   Jack Tootson

ACKNOWLEDGMENTS

We would like to extend our gratitude to the people who added value to this project in a variety of ways. First, to Oscar Fellows and Angela Malek for their suggestions on how to make the content easy to read, to Erika Herndon for conducting the initial research on performance measurement, and to Yvonne O'Brien for contributing the Cost-Benefit Analysis Spreadsheet tool that is used in Chapter Three. We also would like to thank Cool Pages for developing the CD-ROM mini-web site, particularly Shari Reynolds and Michael Scott. We especially benefitted from the contributions of our Jossey-Bass developmental editor, Maryanne Koschier, who found content gaps that we never thought of and for being a strong reader advocate throughout the whole process. We also appreciate the publishing guidance and resource support of Kathleen Dolan-Davies and Matt Holt of Pfeiffer. We also thank the organizations we have worked for over the last twenty years for giving us opportunities to try performance measurement ideas that both failed and succeeded. We have learned so much from our mistakes, and these valuable lessons provided the framework for the global performance measurement system that this book is all about.

Finally, Ferdinand would like to extend his appreciation to his wife, Theresa, and children, Ryne and Rachel, for their inspiration and encouragement and for helping him juggle his priorities effectively during the writing period. Jack would like to thank his wife, Pam, for her love, support, and valuable contributions to the book.

ABOUT THE AUTHORS

Ferdinand Tesoro is currently a measurement and test systems consultant at Dell Learning, Dell Computer Corporation. He and Jack Tootson are currently spearheading the implementation of a global performance measurement system at Dell. Dr. Tesoro has developed a performance measurement process that has been used to evaluate the effectiveness of a variety of training programs, including sales, engineering, software, new hire, leadership, and interpersonal skills. Dr. Tesoro measured whether the training led to on-the-job behavioral change and its impact on productivity, ramp-up time, sales revenue, quota attainment, number of accounts won, and close rate. He has installed such programs for diverse organizations such as Dow Chemical, Shell Oil, and Dell Computer Corporation.

Dr. Tesoro is a member of the Return on Investment (ROI) International Network, American Society for Training and Development, American Society for Quality Control, and International Society for Performance Improvement. As a member of the Evaluation Consortium, he works with cutting-edge measurement and evaluation experts in organizations such as Bell Atlantic, Hewlett-Packard, Microsoft, Dell, Motorola, Xerox, Compaq, Intel, Fidelity Investment, Arthur Andersen, and Allstate Insurance. He completed his Ph.D. in instructional systems design and industrial engineering at Purdue University in 1991. He has been on the faculty of the Training and Development Certification Program and the Human Performance Improvement Certification Workshop at the University of Houston and University of Texas, respectively.

Jack Tootson is the current director for regional operations, Dell Learning, Dell Computer Corporation. As such, he manages the areas of marketing and communications, performance consulting, financial operations, and education services for the Americas (including Canada and Latin America), Europe, Asia-Pacific, and Japan. He is also currently involved with the development of comprehensive competency models for all business segments and lines of businesses at Dell. Mr. Tootson leads the worldwide education planning process for Dell Learning, which integrates measurements with business goals and prioritized performance interventions.

Prior to joining Dell, Mr. Tootson was a senior level executive of Iams Company. He established Iams University and also implemented the Distributor Executive Development Institute, a state-of-the-art program that assists principals with business issues. Mr. Tootson also previously worked for Sargent & Lundy Engineers, CNA Insurance, and GTE as marketing training manager and served as special assistant to the Inspector General, Department of Health and Human Services, Washington, D.C.

Mr. Tootson has served on the editorial boards for *Corporate University Review, Corporate University Exchange,* and the *Academy of Management Executive* publications. He is a member of the International Society for Performance Improvement, American Society for Training and Development, Academy of Management, and National Press Club. He attended the human resources development doctoral program at George Washington University and completed his master's degree in education at Northern Illinois University.

IMPLEMENTING GLOBAL PERFORMANCE MEASUREMENT SYSTEMS

INTRODUCTION

The Need for Performance Measurement

Through our experience in a variety of work environments as leaders and consultants, we have realized that one of the key ingredients of business success has been the ability of organizations to leverage performance-based measurement as a competitive advantage. To sustain success, maintain high productivity levels, retain employees, and keep customers, an organization must know its weaknesses in order to improve its overall performance. Diagnosing performance gaps and implementing initiatives to address performance problems are imperative for organizational effectiveness.

This book introduces a simple four-stage performance measurement process that can provide your organization with a competitive advantage. It is easy to follow and identifies the specific deliverables that you need to complete in each stage. The deliverables are provided as tools and templates for you to use in your organization. A comprehensive case study is also discussed to illustrate application of the tools and templates in an actual business situation.

How This Book Is Organized

We have organized the book in the following way:

Overview. The first chapter of the book provides an overview of performance measurement, including basic definitions, related concepts, and the value of performance measurement in running a business. The second chapter describes the four steps of what we call the "cookbook approach" to performance measurement and lists deliverables for each step. An assessment tool is included here so you can determine the pieces you still need to implement a performance measurement system effectively.

Descriptions and Tools. The rest of the chapters provide a discussion of each of the four stages of performance measurement and the tools that can be used to complete each stage. The purpose of each tool, the steps in developing it, and some tips on how to customize it for your organization are given. Templates of each tool are provided so that you can use them as is or revise them to meet your needs.

Case Study. A third element of the book involves a running case study discussion that applies the cookbook process and illustrates how the tools can be used to implement a performance measurement system, using a fictitious organization. The case study is introduced after Chapter One and incorporated after Chapters Two through Six, illustrating the points from these chapters.

CD-ROM. The final element of the book presents a summary on CD-ROM of the process, the tools, downloadable templates, and case study discussions, designed to simulate a web site. The tools and templates on the CD-ROM have been used and validated by the authors over the years as they have designed and implemented many global performance measurement systems.

Guidelines for Using the Book

Our experiences in different leadership and consultant positions in diverse organizations in the different areas of performance measurement provide the foundation for the book. Writing the book gave us an opportunity to integrate our experiences in a coherent way as a systemic and systematic process. If fully integrated into real-life business processes, a performance measurement system is critical for the success of the business.

The tools, templates, and examples we share in this book reflect our experiences in different organizations with varying cultures and organizational goals. The use of these tools in your organization is not a guarantee for success. Rather, it provides a well-founded and experience-proven thought process to follow when dealing with the issues in performance measurement. As a line manager, HRD consultant, or performance consultant, you can understand your organization—its vision, goals, culture, people, and internal and external environment—so you will know whether these tools will fit or not. You may have to customize the processes and templates provided here for your organization.

Using the CD-ROM

The CD-ROM included with this book is designed to simulate a mini-web site. You can click on selected buttons to access the content as though you were online. The major sections you will find on the CD-ROM's simulated "web site" are:

- *Process.* The performance measurement system, system criteria, measurement process, and assessment tools.
- *Deliverables.* Descriptions of the fifteen tools that are used for the performance measurement process.
- *Downloadables.* Templates for each tool that you can customize for your own organization.
- *Case Study.* Refers to the case study discussion and illustrates how the tools are actually used in the case.

Even if you have the framework, all the templates, and the tools for implementing a performance measurement system, it is not a guarantee for success. However, your efforts will be more likely to be successful and valuable if you understand how to customize everything for your particular organization.

CHAPTER ONE

OVERVIEW OF PERFORMANCE MEASUREMENT

In this chapter, we will lay the groundwork for your understanding of performance measurement systems by providing basic definitions, an historical perspective of measurement, the benefits of performance measurement, and the general flow of the system. We will introduce the global performance measurement system we developed and describe its components. Finally, we will discuss what objections your clients or senior management may have to this system and help you find ways to obtain "buy-in" for implementing a performance measurement system of your own.

Before we proceed further, ask anyone what thoughts come to mind when he or she thinks about performance measurement. The chances are pretty good that you will hear one or more of the following responses:

Situation 1:   "I receive too much data and information. I receive piles of sales and financial reports every day, and I don't know which data really matter to my clients or my management team."

Situation 2:   "I don't know what to measure and where to find the data. We are a nonprofit organization, and it's hard to identify the things that can help us run our business better. Nobody is tracking anything here."

Situation 3:   "I don't know how to do it. I'm in marketing and I would like to know the impact of our advertising efforts on our company's performance. I have read a lot of books about it, but I haven't found a simple, step-by-step process to follow. I just don't know where to begin."

Situation 4:   "It is very difficult to do. The people on my public relations team don't have the statistics and academic background to do it. It's just too complicated. I especially don't understand the financial costing part."

Situation 5:   "I manage a small firm of fifteen people. We don't have the bandwidth nor the resources to implement performance measurement. If we grow to about fifty people, maybe we'll begin looking at it."

Situation 6:   "It takes too much time and effort. Our sales department is stretched to the limit. We don't have the time to collect metrics. We have quotas, and achieving our target sales volume is our top priority."

Situation 7:   "I don't have the people and financial resources in accounting to do it. It is too costly to do, and accounting costs already make up too much of the overhead."

Situation 8:   "My clients haven't asked for it. In human resources, we are expected to recruit, select, provide benefits, train, and evaluate our employees. Management doesn't expect us to provide performance measures. That's the supervisor's responsibility."

Situation 9:   "It's not necessary in product engineering. Our job is to develop the most energy-efficient products for our company. I just don't see the value in conducting performance measurement. How do you measure innovation and creativity anyway?"

Situation 10:   "How can I think of performance measurement? I can't even get my client's commitment to attend the training programs I've developed. I scheduled several courses just last week. The classes were booked solid, but only half of those enrolled showed up."

Sound familiar? Even the most experienced measurement person still hears these reactions often. And you probably even hear it from people you thought "got it."

If you manage any of the departments mentioned in the situations above—sales, public relations, marketing, finance, engineering, human resources, or training— or a nonprofit organization or a government agency, you've probably seen attempts at measuring organizational effectiveness before. You've probably been in one or all of the situations described earlier, and probably some others. Just how *do* you measure the effectiveness of your product-marketing campaigns? The increase in your sales revenues versus the number of new customers? Number of big, new accounts won or number of existing accounts grown? And what is your team's return for investing in these campaigns?

As a manager of people or human resources, you may be charged with the responsibility to use or introduce a performance measurement system. If so, your first job is to educate yourself about performance measurement.

Definition of Performance Measurement

Clarifying assumptions and defining performance measurement are a good place to start. It is important that you and your clients, whether internal or external, agree on the definition and terminology so there is a level playing field. What exactly is performance measurement?

Performance measurement is a process of developing indicators that report on the accomplishments and progress of an organization (Performance Measurement, 1997, May 10). It includes both the setting of targets for desired performance and the review of performance against these targets. Of course, to gauge performance accurately, you must collect and evaluate information that is truly indicative of performance.

Say you work in a computer sales company and your sales team's quota for next year has been increased by 30 percent. As the sales manager, you know that your management team will not agree to hire additional sales representatives to achieve the 30 percent goal. You decide that your best bet is to increase the quota of each person on your sales team, in proportion to each one's current job level and experience. Then you wonder what performance measures you should track to indicate progress toward the established goal.

One basic indicator is business volume, measured in gross sales revenues. This will tell you whether you are actually increasing your business. Another is profit margin, the net proceeds of all the organized human effort and ingenuity that make up your company. Did you make money? Digging deeper into the details that separate direct costs from indirect costs, you can look at the close rate (number of sales closed versus number of sales attempted). How is your salesforce doing?

Now, by using these three measures, you will be able to track the performance of your salesforce on a continuous basis and to establish a regular reporting frequency—daily, weekly, monthly or quarterly—that is appropriate for the growth you desire.

You can also provide real-time feedback and coaching to those who are having difficulty achieving their target quotas. Through analyzing trends, peaks, and valleys in the performance of each of your sales representatives, you can find out the causes of fluctuations in their performance. You can also take corrective action in a timely fashion. If indicators are monitored frequently enough, say on a daily basis, it also provides you with the opportunity to gauge finite sales trends, such as the days of the week when sales are routinely slow, and to identify causes and take whatever steps are necessary to increase productivity.

The value of timely feedback is especially important in fast-paced, high-tech companies. Current Internet technologies enable products to be ordered online and the status of the order, ship dates, and payments to be tracked easily. Providing immediate feedback is a key customer service initiative that has improved customer satisfaction for many organizations.

Purpose of Performance Measurement

Performance consultants and human resource professionals in the companies we have worked with use performance measurement systems in a number of ways, including: (1) to gauge success in achieving goals; (2) to provide recommendations for organizational change; (3) to give feedback to management; and (4) to assess internal inputs and outcomes. Each is discussed below.

To Gauge Success in Achieving Goals. The key to effective performance measurement is to identify the unique measures that can gauge the health and efficiency of your business operations and to use the information you glean to take appropriate actions. The measures vary from organization to organization, even from department to department. One of the measures that was used to determine the effectiveness of the salesforce in the previous example was gross revenues. If you learned that gross sales were lower than expected in the second quarter and that you would fall short of the 30 percent increase in new sales, you might decide to examine gross revenues for each sales team and the close rate to see whether your goals might be too ambitious.

When you looked at individual sales teams, you might find that gross revenues were not equal for all sales teams. One sales team in particular might be doing very poorly with respect to its target sales goal, although conditions are similar and it has approximately the same number of sales opportunities. You would want to find out why.

Next you would look at your second indicator, the team members' individual close rates. You might find out that two members of the team seldom close a sale. Eureka! This is the source of your problem. Now it is necessary to focus on a remedy. First you will have to examine the salespeoples' individual data very carefully. Appropriate measures have helped you identify where the problems are and they will help you as you develop remedial strategies.

To Provide Recommendations for Organizational Change. After you have established operating goals and tactics, measure actual achievement against them and re-examine them in light of the results. Occasionally, the first remedial actions you try will fail. Perhaps your first perceptions were wrong, in which case your solutions would not rectify the situation. Perhaps the reason salespeople do not close deals is the fact that they don't ask the right questions. Perhaps customers are turned off by their style. Are they rewarded for increasing their close rate? Do they lack knowledge about the products that they are selling? By asking many questions, you can systematically identify the root cause of the problem. This is the way that performance measurement is used to guide organizational change and development. It can be used to provide objective, factual data to make more informed day-to-day decisions in running your organization.

To Give Feedback to Management. The real value of performance measurement becomes apparent when business decisions have to be made in a hurry. If a crisis rears its ugly head, you are equipped to provide support and encouragement. Internet and other electronic technologies can now give managers up-to-the-minute information on sales volume, inventory levels, cash flow, accounts receivable, stock value, delivery dates, shipping carriers, availability of personnel, projected direct costs, and overhead. The business software in use today automatically updates the entire system every time someone makes an entry. Depending on the size of the company, updates once consumed hundreds of hours per year, and information (sometimes no more than crude estimates) took at least twenty-four hours to run on the mainframe.

When you've established a good system for communicating performance feedback, managers can make business decisions quickly and objectively.

To Assess Internal Inputs and Outcomes. Performance measurement provides an objective view of the efficiency and effectiveness of the organization as a system. For example, you may be achieving your target numbers on gross revenues but you may not know at what expense. Are your employees working more hours than they should? Are you receiving more customer complaints as a result? Identify the measures to use to gain a more "balanced" view of performance.

In a customer service organization we have worked with, performance of technical support technicians was initially measured in terms of call volume (number of calls per day) and service call time (length of time per call). After analyzing the numbers and trends for the different support teams, we asked team managers whether they were tracking other metrics. We specifically asked for data such as repeat calls from a customer, problem resolution rates (number of customer problems solved versus total number of opportunities), and parts dispatch rates (number of times parts were dispatched versus number of calls). We explained to the managers that call volume and call time alone do not reflect true performance. When we listened to actual calls, we noticed that the support staff tried to answer questions hastily, troubleshoot issues haphazardly, and dispatch parts indiscriminately. When we started to track the repeat calls, resolution rates, and dispatch rate, we found that there was a direct correlation between call volume and repeat calls. Because technicians were expected to increase call volume, they sacrificed customer satisfaction and effective service in the process.

Performance Measurement Systems

A practical performance measurement system is composed of three simple elements: (1) a set of metrics and indicators; (2) a reporting process and delivery tool; and (3) a diagnostic and analysis tool. Figure 1.1 is a visual representation of such a performance measurement system. The elements are briefly described below.

Metrics and Indicators. An interrelated set of indicators must be in place to gauge the effectiveness of a process or outcome and facilitate internal comparisons of an organization's performance over time. Examples of measures to track include sales revenue, cycle time, service time per customer, number of accident-free days, and total dollar donations.

Reporting Process and Delivery Tool. Regular, periodic examination of the indicators is necessary to recognize trends and patterns and to plan appropriate actions. Report on sales, inventory, accounting, and other departmental data in a succinct, abbreviated format that permits managers to examine the relevant information at a glance. The data can be presented in various formats, including hard copy, oral presentations, electronic bulletin boards, and on the web.

FIGURE 1.1. A PERFORMANCE MEASUREMENT SYSTEM

Diagnostic and Analysis Tool. A document is needed that helps people to interpret the data, compares projected results with actual results, and lists any recommendations for performance improvement. This tool usually presents an analysis of the results in terms of contribution to business goals. Correlations between items and trend analysis are examples of techniques that you can use to present your recommendations.

The objective of a performance measurement system is to provide timely access to current, reliable, and relevant information in order to make decisions related to performance improvement. In most sales organizations we have worked with, managers and other decision makers have tools to show them how their teams and individual direct reports are doing relative to key indicators such as revenues and quota attainment. These hard-copy reports are usually provided at the start of every week. Run rates (what will happen if a trend continues) that are less than 100 percent are either highlighted or marked with a red flag to indicate the need for the sales manager to coach those sales representatives who need it.

It goes without saying that the information must reach the right people at the right time in order to be an effective tool and that these people act on the recommendations that the tool generates for them.

Criteria for a Performance Measurement System

For a performance measurement system to have credibility and functionality, it has to meet the criteria described in Table 1.1, which provides recommendations for

TABLE 1.1. CRITERIA FOR A PERFORMANCE MEASUREMENT SYSTEM

Criterion	Recommended Actions
Validity	Select performance measures that your business users value and use for guiding and supporting decisions and/or those that directly align with your organization's goals.
Accuracy and Precision	Your system will only be as good as the data that is in it. Make an effort to ensure that the data you are using is accurate. You also need to leverage existing technology and tools so you can provide real-time access to the most current data to your users.
Completeness or Collective Exhaustiveness	Your performance measurement system should provide your users the capability to drill down to details when needed. It should present a complete picture, so do your homework and cover your bases.
Uniqueness or Mutual Exclusiveness	Make sure your system is different from other reports that your organization produces. The unique and most powerful aspect of a performance measurement system is its ability to

provide meaning and relevance to its users, as well as its prescriptive diagnosis of the data. Users have to be able to identify what they need to do or change based on the information given.

Reliability

Your system has to be simple, scalable, and replicable so that users will trust it. Leveraging existing tools and technology, as well as using a systematic diagnostic process, can enhance its reliability.

Comprehensibility

The data has to be presented so that the users can understand it and do something about it. Do your homework by talking to all your prospective users/clients so that you can meet their needs in terms of format, structure, fields, and other data presentation requirements.

Ability to Be Quantitative

Your performance measurement system should be able to present both quantitative and qualitative data. This guarantees that you will meet the needs of your diverse users—the analytical ones who prefer to look at numbers in structured formats and those who like to read textually presented information. And of course, quantitative data makes comparative analysis easy.

Controllability/ Ownership

Make sure that you identify the content owners for the measures in your system. This is important because if they don't perform their responsibilities, the data in your system becomes inaccurate. Don't give your content owners extra work in feeding data into your system; instead, utilize existing reports that they need to do anyway as part of their jobs and design your measures according to these standard formats.

Flexibility

Provide flexibility to your users by giving them reporting options. You may have standard reports that meet common needs of your users, but provide them with options so they can customize reports to fit their needs. There are various technology tools that can provide this capability. See Chapter Five for more information on technology and tools.

Cost Effectiveness

To implement a cost-effective system, leverage existing technologies and reporting procedures, streamline lists of measures, and utilize existing databases. Solicit organization-wide support so user operating and maintenance costs are minimized.

Adaptability

The performance measurement system should be scalable so that it can adapt to changes in priorities, business initiatives, and performance measures.

Maintainability

This is key to the success of your performance measurement system. Make sure you have a solid maintenance plan for keeping your data current, relevant, and valid. Solicit commitment to content ownership up-front by providing data owners with "what's in it for them" benefits.

addressing each of these criteria while building a performance measurement system.

When we developed a performance measurement system for a computer sales organization, we first determined which criteria were deemed important by our clients. The top three factors we found were validity, accuracy, and flexibility. Our clients wanted accurate reports that came from credible sources and that could be presented in various formats.

Measurement Versus Evaluation

In our experience, clients often confuse evaluation with measurement. Let's look at the differences, especially in terms of how they are used for performance improvement. It is important to understand this difference, as we are discussing measurement throughout this book, not evaluation.

Evaluation

Worthen and Sanders (1987) define evaluation as *the formal determination of the quality, effectiveness, or value of a program, product, process, objective, or curriculum*. It is the collection and analysis of data; the goal is to provide useful information for decision making. For example, end-of-the-course evaluations are given to learners in order to provide instructors with feedback on how well the course was received.

Hale (1998) describes evaluation as *the act of judging something or placing a value on it*. Value, however, is relative. Your job as a human resource consultant or performance measurement expert is to question clients and listen to their answers to find out what is valuable to them. In other words, you don't put value on the product, process, or goal; your client does.

For example, in a profit-driven company, management will evaluate your effectiveness through measures that mean most to them—probably profit metrics such as profit margin, margin percent, average selling price, and revenues. This is especially so if executives are rewarded for their performance in these areas.

For a customer service organization, the key measures would be customer satisfaction ratings, first-time-fix rates, or others that are integral in running the core business—providing excellent customer service.

Measurement

Measurement, on the other hand, is the act of comparing. When clients talk about "improving" performance, they want to close the gap between current performance and a standard or goal they have set. Measurement is done by gathering information about a situation, activity, or process and then comparing that information against a set of criteria. In nonprofit organizations, performance of local affiliates is usually measured against national standards and criteria. Depending on the size of the target population and potential contributions, each local team may set higher goals than the national organization has set. The point is that local offices determine how well they do relative to their own pre-set standards and criteria. If they exceed their goals, then their performance is considered excellent. If they do not meet their expectations, then there are opportunities for improvement.

Figure 1.2 shows a gap analysis to find the difference between current and desired performance. As human resource and performance consultants, your job is to find out whether your clients have considered all the available information and to determine what criteria should be used as a basis for comparison (Hale, 1998).

Gaps are measured in terms of how much improvement is needed to accomplish the goals of the business. In the example in Figure 1.2, customer satisfaction ratings have to improve by 12 percent. How to determine reasonable targets will be discussed in Chapter Four.

Based on the definitions above, measurement—not evaluation—is the vehicle that performance consultants, HR professionals, and line managers use to assess their effectiveness. For performance improvement to occur, baseline data and target goals have to be clearly identified; otherwise, there is no basis for comparison and you would not know whether improvement had really occurred.

For purposes of this book, measurement will be consistently used to reflect performance improvement. For example, an increase in close rate (the ratio of calls

FIGURE 1.2. PERFORMANCE GAP ANALYSIS

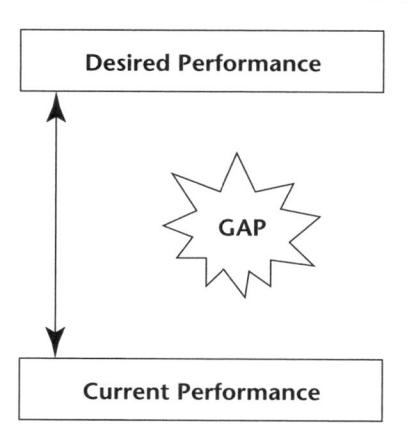

Examples
95% customer satisfaction rating
30% penetration rate
$50k contribution per sponsor

12% improvement in customer satisfaction
10% improvement in penetration rate
$20k improvement in contribution per sponsor

Examples
83% customer satisfaction rating
20% penetration rate
$30k contribution per sponsor

to number sold) of 5 percent means performance of sales employees in "closing sales" has improved by 5 percent, as measured by some reliable means.

What Performance Measurement Is Not

Certain terms are often used in reference to performance measurement. For the purposes of this book, they are defined below to clearly distinguish them from performance measurement *(How to Measure Performance: A Handbook of Techniques and Tools)*.

- *Baselining.* The process of establishing a reference set of data that reflects the *current* state of a process, system, or product.
- *Benchmarking.* A method of measuring a process, system, or outcome within an organization against those of a recognized leader in the field. The purpose of benchmarking is to provide a target for improved performance.
- *Best in Class.* Leader or top performer in relation to a particular performance goal as identified through a benchmark.
- *Effectiveness.* The ability to accomplish a desired result or to fulfill a purpose or intent.
- *Efficiency:* The quality or degree of effective operations as measured against cost, resources, and time.
- *Re-engineering.* A process of rethinking and redesigning work processes to achieve noticeable improvements in response to customer needs and/or to achieve significant reductions in cost.
- *Standards.* A prescribed set of rules, conditions, or requirements used to measure or define the quality or quantity of particular performance elements.
- *Value-added.* Process or steps that enhance an outcome.

A Global Performance Measurement System (GPMS)

Most of the organizations we have worked with do not see performance measurement systems as systemic and systematic approaches. But they are systemic because how you leverage the results depends on whether you have identified the right key indicators. Performance measurement systems also involve a structured process: (1) knowing your organization's goals, (2) determining success factors, and (3) assessing whether the strategies you implemented were successful.

A "global" performance measurement system (GPMS) presents a *comprehensive and encompassing view* of performance across an organization. Although the focus of this book is on global performance measurement systems, nonglobal, nonprofit, and small organizations can benefit from the systematic and systemic approach presented here to improve their own performance. The essential elements (metrics and indicators, reporting tools, and diagnostic tools) can be applied in any type of organization. Performance consultants, HR professionals, and line managers can also use this process, as it is universal.

A GPMS includes performance metrics that not only reflect desired organizational outcomes but also process, departmental, team, and individual measures. For large organizations with an international presence, the global performance measurement system should include unique regional performance measures. Otherwise, comparing international operations with U.S. operations will generate false conceptions. For example, European countries have different labor laws, taxes, and overhead, and employee benefits are usually different from American-based firms, so it is very important to determine the regional factors that are related to performance.

Value and Role of GPMS

The real value of the system presented in this book is not the deliverables nor the templates, but rather what you will learn about aligning performance measurement with the goals of your organization. This is a great benefit from using the global performance measurement approach. Here are some of the benefits to you and your organization from using this approach:

Strategic Planning. The system facilitates development of strategic and tactical plans for the organization, department, or team. It can provide information that identifies performance gaps so that business strategies can be developed. For example, you could discover in which regional areas or departments the potential for increasing market share is the greatest or which region has the lowest average selling price. The answers to these and other questions can be provided by a good global performance measurement system. A natural by-product of strategic and tactical business plans is a list of measures and indicators that reflect progress in accomplishment of these plans.

Linking Performance and Business Metrics. The system provides an opportunity to link departmental/unit metrics to organization-wide metrics. The GPMS provides its audiences with an opportunity to make connections and correlations between different categories. For example, data can be used to identify the relationship between sales revenues and close rate or the correlation between customer satisfaction and profit margin.

Central Source of Information. The system gives a central source for all metrics and the ability to access and compare performance of units or departments. This reduces the probability of having redundant, ill-defined, and inconsistent metrics. For highly decentralized organizations, a common repository is needed to establish a consistent measurement language and common yardsticks.

Customized Metric Needs. The system enables metrics and reports to be customized. With the use of the latest reporting technology, you can provide your audience with ad hoc and custom reporting capability. For example, a human resource manager in Europe can select measures and design reports based on a common, organizational database. The management of each region may value measures differently, depending on the gap that needs to be closed. If, for example, the major priority for a region is to increase market share by acquiring new accounts, sales revenues and profit margin may be secondary goals. Increasing margins and average selling price can be the top priority for other regions that have established themselves in the marketplace.

Consistency and Ease of Use. Consistent, easy-to-use reporting formats are especially important. A GPMS can be designed to include standard, consistent reports on a regular basis. For example, weekly reports on revenues, margins, and close rates of sales representatives can be produced by a GPMS. Custom and client-specific metrics can also be built into the system.

Comparative Analysis. The capability of doing comparative data analysis is another feature of the system. For example, comparisons can be made between forecast and actual for budgets, revenues, quota attainment, and average selling price.

Instant Reports. Status reports can be generated quickly for presentations, reviews, and training plans. The use of a database-driven and web-based reporting tool can allow audiences easy and timely access to financial, sales, and customer service performance reports.

How to Sell Performance Measurement in Your Organization

Table 1.2 can serve as a guide for obtaining commitment from your organization to implement a performance measurement system. Ways to position and market a system are given in the table. Know your audience. Understand their priorities and interests so you can leverage them during the discussion. For example, project managers may care only about strategies that can improve performance; department managers

TABLE 1.2. WAYS TO SELL PERFORMANCE MEASUREMENT IN YOUR ORGANIZATION

Possible Audience	Objection/Challenge	Framework for Responding
Project managers and consultants	• I don't know how to do it. • It takes a lot of time and effort. • It is too complex. • It is very difficult to do. • I don't have the resources nor the expertise to do it.	There is a new, simple, cookbook approach that you can use in any type of organization, from auto dealerships to nonprofit businesses, that will walk you through the process. It comes with easy-to-use templates and tools that make performance measurement easy to implement. The tools also include tips on how to customize the content to meet the needs of your business.
Staff—HR, Training, Performance Consulting, Line Management	• It is not a priority. • I don't know what to measure. • I get too much data and information. • I don't know the metrics that my organization values.	If you can define your business and operational goals, you have already described the critical elements for analyzing your performance. These are the basic measures that matter. After defining these goals, you can break them down into relevant indicators by department or functional area.
Managers and Executives	• I don't know the value that this brings to the organization. • It is a waste of time and effort. • My business is too small. We don't need it.	In any business or operation, you need to know how well you are doing with regard to your actual potential. You need to know the things that truly affect your operation and how to cope with changes. Performance measurement is about understanding your business. Success seldom happens by accident.

may be mainly concerned about efficiency, cost, time, and resources; and the staff of the department may be held accountable for the success of all of these projects.

When any of the situations that were listed at the beginning of the chapter come up, use the table for responding to objections. The various audiences are listed in the first column; their typical objections are in the second column; and a suggested response is sketched out in the third column. Make sure to expand on this framework and add organization-specific goals, programs, strategies, and initiatives to drive home your points.

Use this book as your resource to make things happen. It is a guide to the processes and tools for successfully implementing a global performance measurement system.

Other Models in Performance Measurement

Traditional performance measurement approaches focus on desired outcomes and outputs. For performance measurement to be seen as a critical factor in accomplishing organizational goals, it has to establish the link between desired performance and outcome measures clearly. It also should include process and input measures to provide a balanced view of performance. This means that, although your goals may reflect the outcomes you want to achieve (such as increasing market share by 15 percent), your measurement system should not only include measures that track whether you are getting there, but also those that show how you are achieving those outcomes.

For example, in a service-based organization, your desired outcomes may be high customer satisfaction and excellent customer service, but you also need to track process measures such as service time and first-time-fix rate. High customer satisfaction can be because too much time is being spent with customers or the customers may have had to call five times before a problem is fixed. The satisfaction may have been achieved at the expense of efficiency and effectiveness.

Two of the most widely used models for measuring performance are described below.

Kirkpatrick's Four Levels of Evaluation

Kirkpatrick's (1967) model has been used as a starting point for performance measurement in many organizations to evaluate the effectiveness of training and other performance improvement programs. However, the model shows effectiveness outcomes and does not describe how to implement them. The model describes four levels of measures:

1. *Reaction.* How well did the employees like the program?
2. *Learning.* To what extent did they learn the facts, principles, and knowledge that were taught during the program?
3. *Behavior.* To what extent did their job behavior change because of the program?
4. *Results.* What final organizational results were achieved?

As a performance or training consultant, you still must establish a system that includes assessing gaps and generating valid, objective recommendations. For example, if reaction ratings average 4.2 on a five-point scale, do you modify the program design or change the instructors? You can't tell! You need a system and a process that provide you with other measures, such as percentage of class that belongs to the target audience, to give you reasons for the recommendations you make. You cannot make recommendations to change design and instructor delivery solely on reaction ratings.

Table 1.3 shows the differences between Kirkpatrick's evaluation levels in terms of the value of the information, power to show results, frequency of use, and level of difficulty in conducting the measurement. Level 1 data, such as reactions to content or instructor, are not as valuable as Level 4 data on changes in revenues or profit margin. Although reaction data is considered the least valuable, it is the most frequently collected. Business results are the most difficult to assess and validate because of the need to use scientific methods to ensure validity and reliability of the data.

The key point here is that if Kirkpatrick's model is ingrained in your training and performance consulting organization then, by all means, use it. But don't stop there. The real value of these evaluation results is how they are leveraged to assess performance gaps and identify the effectiveness of your performance improvement efforts.

Input-Process-Output-Outcome Measurement Model

In her latest publication, *The Performance Consultant's Fieldbook,* Judith Hale (1998) presents a measurement model that evaluates how work gets done and whether an intervention or program has made a difference. Hale's model describes measures that not only reflect outcomes but also the efficiency and optimization of resources used. The categories of the model are defined below:

1. *Inputs.* Measures about what people in the job have to deal with. Examples include volume, complexity, clarity, and maturity.
2. *Processes.* Measures about how people do the task. Examples include response time, cycle time, efficiency, and cost.

TABLE 1.3. DIFFERENCES AMONG FOUR LEVELS OF EVALUATION

Chain of Impact	Value of Information	Power of Results	Frequency of Use	Difficulty of Assessment
Reaction (Level 1)	Least Valuable	Least Power	Frequent	Easy
Learning (Level 2)				
Behavior (Level 3)				
Results (Level 4)	Most Valuable	Most Power	Infrequent	Difficult

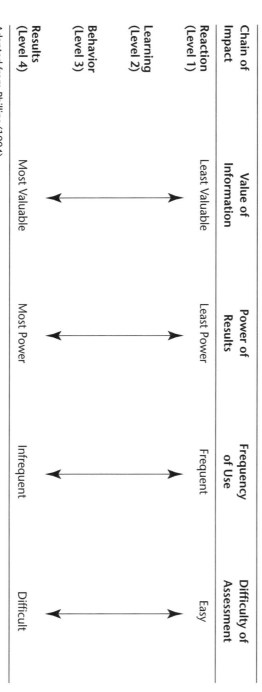

Adapted from Phillips (1994).

3. *Outputs.* Measures about how much people did. Examples include quantitative measures, customers serviced, and worth.
4. *Outcomes.* Measures about results or consequences of what people did. Examples include satisfaction, accomplishment, aftermath, cost, compliance, and image.

Hale's model enhances Kirkpatrick's four levels of evaluation in the following ways:

- It provides a bigger picture view of performance measurement by not only dealing with outcomes but also with inputs and process measures.
- It provides context about the intervention or program and differentiates according to work volume, level of complexity, clarity of information, and customer maturity. This helps the customer or business client understand the situation better and puts the results in a new perspective.
- It reflects process efficiencies (time, cost, effort), while Kirkpatrick's levels deal solely with outcomes. It provides balance between effectiveness and efficiency.

When designing a measurement strategy, you must provide a balanced set of measures that not only includes results and outcomes (the what's) but also communicates the limiting constraints and process efficiencies (the how's) in achieving the goals. Results and numbers do not tell the whole story; using a balanced measurement approach provides an objective rationale behind the numbers. In the sales organizations we have worked with, most sales managers only track measures such as revenues, quota attainment, and profit margin. These are only short-term indicators. Measures such as close rate, customer satisfaction ratings, and accuracy percentage of customer orders are long-term indicators that lead to repeat business and building relationships with customers. A comprehensive discussion of balanced measurement scorecards is provided in Chapter Four of this book.

In small organizations, business outcome measures such as liquidity, profitability, and growth should be balanced with process efficiency and effectiveness measures. Examples of the latter are cycle time, cost, and account retention. The company cannot afford to have the desired outcome measures at the expense of efficiency. If a company exceeds its outcome measures for the month, yet receives a significant number of customer complaints because of the haphazard service it provided, chances are it won't be getting a lot of repeat business. The company achieves its goal in the short term, but loses in the long run. By using more credible, well-grounded measurement methods, you can help the company achieve a higher level of all-around performance.

◆ ◆ ◆

Key Summary Points

The following are the key points emphasized in this chapter.

1. Performance measurement is essential to the success of an organization and can be used as an effective means of improving performance.
2. A performance measurement system consists of measures or indicators; a reporting process tool such as the web or hard copy reports; and a diagnostic tool that describes performance implications of the data.
3. The criteria for an effective performance measurement system include validity, accuracy and precision, completeness or collective exhaustiveness, uniqueness or mutual exclusiveness, reliability, comprehensibility, ability to be quantitative, controllability or ownership, flexibility, cost effectiveness, adaptability, and maintainability.
4. The key to setting up an effective global performance measurement system is the acquisition of relevant data in a brief, targeted format.
5. For a performance measurement system to be truly effective, it should include indicators that provide a balanced view of performance. This includes using input-process-outcome-output measures (Hale, 1998) that reflect effectiveness and efficiency.

APPLICATION EXERCISE: CASE STUDY

To ensure application of theories and tools presented in this book, each succeeding chapter will include application exercises. A single, comprehensive case study will be used throughout the book so that you have concrete examples showing how the steps in the cookbook process are followed. The case study also makes sure that you fully experience an integrated performance measurement approach that is strongly tied to the needs of your organization.

The case study for FJT Tech Company is described below. Additional information to the case will be provided as needed in the succeeding chapters. You will be asked to answer the case study questions in each chapter to assess how you apply the theories and tools you have learned. The answers to the case study questions, including how the tools were used at FJT Tech, are also discussed in each chapter.

A Global Performance Measurement System for FJT Tech Company

FJT Tech Company manufactures, sells, and supports digital communication devices (Training Impact Group, 1998). The company's corporate headquarters is located in Colorado with regional offices in the Americas (including Canada and Latin America), Europe, Asia-Pacific, and Japan. Manufacturing operations are centralized in Colorado and Brazil (Americas), Scotland (Europe), Indonesia and China (Asia-Pacific and Japan), with sales and service personnel also housed in these locations. It has approximately 16,000 employees worldwide. Last year, annual revenue of FJT Tech was $10 billion.

FJT Tech's organizational mission is to dominate the market in wireless digital communications devices by providing state-of-the-art products at reasonable prices to the consumer.

FJT Tech's learning and performance organization has its corporate headquarters based in Colorado. The centralized services available in corporate include instructional design, performance technology, testing and certification, program management, and administrative services. Each of the company's different business units such as sales, manufacturing, customer support, finance, etc., as well as each regional office, has its own performance improvement team. These teams funnel their training and other performance needs to the corporate office. Corporate then deploys a project team that analyzes, designs, and develops solutions that address these needs. The corporate and regional teams collaboratively implement and deliver the solutions.

Business Problem

A competitor surprised FJT Tech last week by announcing the avail-ability of a new digital wireless phone that weighs only 2 ounces. Its functionality and price are the same as FJT Tech's current 5-ounce model. The product announcement was accompanied by an adver-tising blitz in print and on TV. Market share for new sales for FJT Tech went down by 8 percentage points this week. Average weekly rev-enues per sales representative went down from $45K to $30K. On an annual basis, this would translate to a $30M revenue loss.

FJT Tech's executive team believes that to maintain its competi-tive advantage, the company must respond aggressively to the com-petitor's action. It wants to further increase its market share and increase sales revenues for this product line. To determine the strate-gies for carrying out these goals, the executive team appointed a cross-functional task force composed of representatives from sales, marketing, accounting, human resources, product engineering, and the learning organization.

The Need for a Performance Measurement System at FJT Tech

As the lead performance consultant in FJT Tech's learning organiza-tion, you've heard that the company's executive team has assigned a cross-functional task force that will address the given business prob-lem and identify strategies for addressing them. You have not been in-vited to the task force's meeting, but your department's VP has recommended that you attend in her behalf. She has also asked you to make sure that performance measurement is integrated in the busi-ness solutions that are generated by this cross-functional group. You are very excited because you realize that the opportunity for imple-menting a performance measurement system at FJT Tech is NOW more than ever.

CHAPTER TWO

A COOKBOOK APPROACH TO PERFORMANCE MEASUREMENT

In this chapter, we will present a simple four-stage process for implementing global performance measurement systems. You will also learn about the different deliverables that you need to complete each stage. An assessment tool for determining how much you know about the performance measurement process is included, as well as a way to interpret your assessment results. Finally, we introduce the case study at the end of this chapter. The case study is the common thread that links all the succeeding chapters. At the end of each chapter, we discuss how the case illustrates different concepts, deliverables, and templates that were covered in that particular chapter.

Our experiences with many organizations that deliver a variety of products and services to customers have provided us with opportunities to build this collection of performance measurement tools. Some of these tools are new, but most have been used many times and have been proven to work well.

Now, let's get down to it. Here is our cookbook approach, which you can implement easily, regardless of your experience or skills in performance measurement.

A Cookbook Approach to Performance Measurement

Here is a four-stage performance measurement process that is simple, easy to use, and practical. The steps are visually presented in Figure 2.1; the specific

FIGURE 2.1. A COOKBOOK APPROACH TO PERFORMANCE MEASUREMENT

Deliverables

Establish the Business Case	List of business goals Prioritized list of goals Strategic council for measurement Business case for measurement Communication and marketing plan
Identify Metrics	List of key metrics Linkage between goals and metrics Performance measurement scorecard Established targets
Implement the System	Framework for tracking data Selecting right media Criteria for selecting technology
Leverage to Improve Performance	Criteria for selecting data format Techniques for presenting data Strategies for leveraging results

deliverables that you need to complete each stage are included. A description of each stage is provided below, along with the key issues to address during each stage.

As outlined in Figure 2.1, the stages in the performance measurement process involve the following:

Establish the Business Case for Measurement. In this stage, you have to research information needed for your business case, produce a document that shows how measurement will help accomplish business goals, and identify a strategy for presenting your case to key decision makers. The key issues you need to address in this step include: (1) determining the prioritized list of business initiatives or goals; (2) developing a performance measurement plan that directly aligns with these goals; and (3) writing communication and marketing plans.

Identify the Metrics That Reflect Key Performance Outcomes. Here, you need to produce a list of key metrics and indicators that you will track and manage. You will also develop tools for collecting information about these indicators. Finally, you will need to identify the sources for the data in your performance measurement system.

Implement the Performance Measurement System. This step involves rolling out a technology-based tool to track and report results for your indicators. The tool also provides a variety of reports to decision makers. The issues that you need to address during this step include: (1) selecting the right media or tool for your system; (2) addressing technology implementation issues; and (3) generating standard or custom report formats for your clients.

Leverage the System to Improve Performance. In this step, you analyze data and present your diagnosis of performance improvement opportunities. The key issues you need to address now are: (1) identifying strategies for analyzing data and (2) diagnosing performance improvement opportunities using fact-based information. Finally, you will generate performance-specific recommendations based on your data. For example, at this point you should know whether performance coaching is needed and what types of data can help you project future performance. This step will help you ask and answer these important questions.

Performance Measurement Assessment Tool

Where do you begin? Try answering the measurement assessment tool in Table 2.1 to find out how much you know about the performance measurement process. This assessment will help you identify gaps in your knowledge and will point toward the appropriate steps that you can take to address them. The tool gives you an overall picture of where you stand as you begin to implement a robust performance measurement system for your organization. Your responses to the assessment tool will tell you, among other things, whether you have identified the "right" metrics, whether you are using the right data analysis method, or whether you have the right prioritized business goals.

TABLE 2.1. PERFORMANCE MEASUREMENT ASSESSMENT TOOL

Below is a checklist of items that comprise a performance measurement system. Please check those items that currently exist or are available in your organization. Then total the checks you have made and fill in the blanks for subtotals and your total assessment score.

_____ 1. Do you have a prioritized list of your key organizational goals/initiatives?

_____ 2. Do you have a formal process for identifying and prioritizing strategic initiatives based on the prioritized goals above?

_____ 3. Do you have a strategic planning committee or business council in place?

_____ 4. Do you have a framework for developing a business case for any strategic initiative or performance improvement proposal?

_____ 5. Do you have a communication and marketing plan for tracking achievement of strategic initiatives?

_____   **Subtotal Score 1 (Add items you checked in numbers 1–5.)**

_____ 6. Do you have a process that directly links your performance improvement initiatives with your organization's business goals?

_____ 7. Do you have a performance measurement scorecard that you use for managing performance?

_____ 8. Do you have access to business, financial, customer service, sales, training, and other metrics in your organization?

_____   **Subtotal Score 2 (Add items you checked in numbers 6–8.)**

_____ 9. Do you currently have baseline data for business, financial, customer service, training, and other metrics in your organization?

_____ 10. Do you have target goals established for each performance measure in your scorecard?

_____ 11. Do you know when to select the right media for communicating your measurement results?

_____ 12. Do you use a technology tool to deliver an integrated performance measurement system?

_____   **Subtotal Score 3 (Add items you checked in numbers 9–12.)**

_____ 13. Do you know what specific techniques to use for presenting your measurement data?

_____ 14. Do you know what specific techniques to use for identifying causes of poor performance?

_____ 15. Do you know what specific techniques to use for determining variables that directly impact excellent performance?

_____   **Subtotal Score 4 (Add items you checked in numbers 13–15.)**

_____   **ASSESSMENT SCORE (Subtotal Scores 1–4)**

Analyzing and Interpreting Your Assessment Results

For practical purposes, your assessment score tells where you stand relative to establishing a performance measurement system. The higher your total score, the better off you are. A score of thirteen or higher indicates you may have the basic elements needed for building your performance measurement system.

Each subtotal represents a step in the cookbook process described earlier and shown in Figure 2.1. Subtotal 1 represents the elements you need for the Establish Business Case step. The subtotal where your score is lowest indicates your highest priority. It is important that you have all the essential elements needed, so you must take action on items you did not check.

Tools for Performance Measurement

Now we're cooking. Now that you know the steps needed to implement your performance measurement process, let's examine the tools you need to ensure that you have all the necessary ingredients for your measurement recipe. A list of the tools and their purposes is provided in Table 2.2.

The succeeding chapters describe each of the four steps in the performance measurement process in great detail. Chapter Three discusses Establishing the Business Case, Chapter Four covers Identifying the Right Performance Metrics, Chapter Five involves Implementing the Performance Management System, and Chapter Six presents Leveraging Results to Improve Performance. You will also learn when, how, and where to use each of the tools listed in Table 2.2.

◆ ◆ ◆

Key Summary Points

The following are the key points covered in this chapter.

1. A simple, easy-to-follow linear approach to performance measurement is needed for practitioners who don't have formal backgrounds and knowledge in the field.
2. The four basic steps in the performance measurement process are: (a) establishing the business case, (b) identifying the right performance metrics, (c) implementing the performance measurement system, and (d) leveraging results to improve performance.
3. To complete the cookbook, tools and templates are identified for each step that make it easy for you to fill in the gaps.

TABLE 2.2. TOOLS FOR PERFORMANCE MEASUREMENT

Tool/ Template	Assessment Question	Purpose of Tool/Template
Step 1: Establish Business Goals [Chapter 3]		
Tool #1— **Performance** **Measurement** **Strategic** **Planning**	1. Do you have a prioritized list of your key organizational goals/initiatives and the measures that signify success of these initiatives?	Ensures that performance improvement efforts are linked with organizational priorities/issues
Tool #2— **Cost-Benefit** **Analysis** **Spreadsheet**	2. Do you have a formal process for identifying and prioritizing strategic initiatives based on the prioritized goals above?	Identifies and prioritizes performance improvement strategies and initiatives
Tool #3— **Strategic** **Council for** **Performance** **Measurement**	3. Do you have a strategic planning committee or business council in place?	Provides business clients opportunity to set strategic direction for performance measurement
Tool #4— **Establishing** **Your Business** **Case**	4. Do you have a framework for developing a business case for any strategic initiative or performance improvement proposal?	Establishes a simple, business-centric justification for performance measure-ment efforts
Tool #5— **Communication** **and Marketing** **Plan**	5. Do you have a communication and marketing plan for tracking achievement of strategic initiatives?	Generates commitment and buy-in to measurement initiatives
Step 2: Identify the Metrics [Chapter 4]		
Tool #6— **Linking Metrics** **with Goals**	6. Do you have a process that directly links performance improvement initiatives with your organization's business goals?	Establishes direct linkage of initiatives with business priorities
Tool #7— **Performance** **Measurement** **Scorecard**	7. Do you have a performance measurement scorecard that you use for managing performance?	Provides a consistent, goal-centered framework for identifying appropriate measures
Tool #8— **Types of** **Department** **and Functional** **Metrics**	8. Do you have access to business, financial, customer service, sales, training, and other metrics in your organization?	Provides examples of kinds of metrics that are tracked in various functional areas of the business

Step 3: Implement the System [Chapter 5]

Tool #9— Determining Baseline and Target Metrics	9. Do you currently have baseline data for business, financial, customer service, training, and other metrics in your organization?	Recommends a template for identifying baseline information for each key measure
Tool #10— Framework for Tracking Performance Data	10. Do you have target goals established for each performance measure in your scorecard?	Recommends a template for establishing targets and goals
Tool #11— Selecting the Right Media for Communicating Results	11. Do you know when to select the right media for communicating your performance results?	Recommends a template for presenting results on key performance measures
Tool #12— Technology Checklist for Measurement Reporting	12. Do you use a technology tool to deliver an integrated performance measurement system?	Identifies criteria for selecting a technology tool to present measurement data

Step 4: Leverage the Results [Chapter 6]

Tool #13— Constructing a Line Graph	13. Do you know when and how to use a line graph for presenting data?	Describes purpose and step-by-step process for constructing line graphs
Tool #14— Constructing a Cause-Effect Diagram	14. Do you know what specific techniques to use for identifying causes of poor performance?	Describes purpose and step-by-step process for identifying causes of poor performance
Tool #15— Constructing a Scatter Diagram	15. Do you know what specific techniques to use for determining variables that directly impact excellent performance?	Describes purpose and step-by-step process for determining variables that improve performance

APPLICATION EXERCISE: CASE STUDY, CHAPTER TWO

POSITIONING A GLOBAL PERFORMANCE MEASUREMENT SYSTEM FOR FJT TECH

Discussion: Questions and Answers

Using the knowledge you have learned in this chapter, here are some questions and their answers that will help you and FJT Tech move strategically forward with this business problem:

1. What value does a performance measurement system bring to FJT Tech?

   A performance measurement system is important if FJT Tech is to remain competitive in what it does. It looks as though the competition has pulled a fast one on the company, and one of the possible reasons is lack of appropriate data that "predicted" this new product. For FJT Tech to move forward and reclaim the market that was lost, it has to establish a global performance measurement system that can help the company run its business better, including forecasting industry trends and developing valid strategic plans.

2. How will you sell the need for a performance measurement system to the cross-functional task force?

   Here are a few questions you need to ask the cross-functional task force so you can effectively position the need for a performance measurement system.

   • What are FJT Tech's business goals now in light of what their competitor did? Reduce or minimize sales losses? Accelerate the introduction of the new product? Increase market share and revenues for the new product?

   • How can they determine whether they are headed in this direction? How will they know that they have completely addressed this strategic concern?

   • How can they prevent this type of thing from happening to them again?

- What metrics will tell them that they are successful with these initiatives?

After you have listened to the team's responses, then you can position how a performance measurement system can address the issues they have raised. Remember, you don't always need to have all the answers.

3. What basic elements do you need to get your performance measurement system project going?

   Using Figure 1.1 in Chapter 1, page 9, to remind yourself of the four essential components that you need:

   - *Determination of the performance gap that needs to be analyzed in solving FJT Tech's business problem and the resulting interventions that will be used to address the causes of the gap.* For example, in the situation at FJT Tech, you could gather information about its product forecasting, market research, and competitor analysis processes and compare the results against a set of criteria that is defined by the cross-functional task force that was assigned to address this business problem. Possible interventions that can come out of this analysis could be product redesign or new product introduction, marketing the redesigned or new product aggressively, and training the sales force to sell the new/redesigned product.

   - *Key indicators and metrics that will signify your success in solving the problem.* For FJT Tech, these key indicators can include market share percentage, which has drastically reduced since the introduction of the competitor's product, and sales revenues. It can also include profit loss or opportunity costs. Finally, FJT Tech needs to assess the impact of the interventions that they will be implementing, such as new product development, marketing new product, and new product sales training, on these key indicators.

   - *A reporting process and methods of delivery of measurement results.* In our experience with a similar situation, we first identified the key business audiences who needed access to these indicators so that they could track ongoing performance. These may include your executives, sales managers and area managers, finance, and marketing. Then, determine the appropriate methods of delivering reports (such as e-mail or hard copy report) and the format of each report (executive summary, detailed results, or report snapshot) that is appropriate for each group.

- *Analysis methods that present your data in meaningful and impactful ways so management can take action and make appropriate decisions.* Detailed examples of analysis methods are covered in Chapter Six of this book. These can give you some ideas on how best to present your data. Methods include data tables, line graph, pie charts, and trend line analysis charts.

4. You have contacted the senior vice president of sales assigned to head the Business Task Force and have asked for 30 minutes to present your case for a performance measurement system. He has reservations about how a performance measurement system can help this business problem, but finally agreed to meet. He also said executives don't have a lot of time and have only 10 minutes to listen to your spiel. Develop a three-paragraph description of what and how you will you share your performance measurement system proposal with this task force using the template below.

CASE STUDY TEMPLATE FOR FJT TECH PRESENTATION

Paragraph 1

I. Present the current situation at FJT Tech:

- New competitive digital wireless phone in the marketplace;

- Subsequent loss of market share and revenues;

- Potential major loss of yearly revenues.

II. Present the solution for a global performance measurement system at FJT Tech.

- Include a brief description of a global performance measurement system (GPMS) from Chapter One.

III. Give the benefits of the GPMS.

- For the present situation include:

1. Monitor current performance.

2. Identify current performance gaps and identify potential interventions to close the gaps.

3. Prevent potential situations similar to what happened with the competitor.

- For future situations, include:

    1. Benchmarking of exemplary performance;

    2. Timely diagnosis of performance problems and identification of coaching opportunities;

    3. Prediction of future performance based on objective measurement data;

    4. Identification of other factors that can improve performance.

Paragraph 2

I. Describe briefly how the solution is implemented.

- Include Figure 2.1 from Chapter Two

- Include the steps on pages 26–27 of Chapter Two:

    1. Establish the business goals for measurement.

    2. Identify the metrics that reflect key performance outcomes.

    3. Implement the performance measurement system.

    4. Leverage the system to improve performance.

II. Describe how the solution is used in other companies (see the example discussed in Chapter Three about how a telephone selling course improved company performance at a sales organization).

III. Acknowledge potential objections to the solution and show ways to overcome potential problems with implementation.

- Include objections from Table 1.2 in Chapter One and expand on the skeletal framework provided as a response to each objection. When possible, consult with colleagues and key allies on appropriate strategies.

Paragraph 3

I. Choose A or B.

A. Present an image of potential dangers to the company if the solution is NOT used.

Examples could be continued loss of market share and revenues, loss of jobs, loss of image and credibility, shareholder disfavor.

OR

B. Present an image of potential rewards to the company if solution is used.

Provide examples such as recapture of market share and revenues, reduction of cost, accelerated design and development of new products.

II. Close with a restatement of the proposed solution, GPMS, and the key benefits of the system for FJT Tech.

CHAPTER THREE

ESTABLISHING THE BUSINESS CASE

How do you show others the value of performance measurement to your business? What are the key business initiatives that your organization has prioritized? How do you establish management commitment and support for your measurement efforts? How do you involve your clients up-front? This chapter will provide you with specific tools and techniques to help you answer all these questions. See the model on this page to remind yourself of where you are in the cookbook model.

As you saw in the case study presented after the previous chapter, one of your first steps to implementing a performance measurement system is to establish its value to the business. Whatever you do, including performance measurement, you need to obtain management's commitment and support first. The only way you can obtain this commitment is if the organization and its management team see the value of what you are doing. Here are the steps you must undertake to

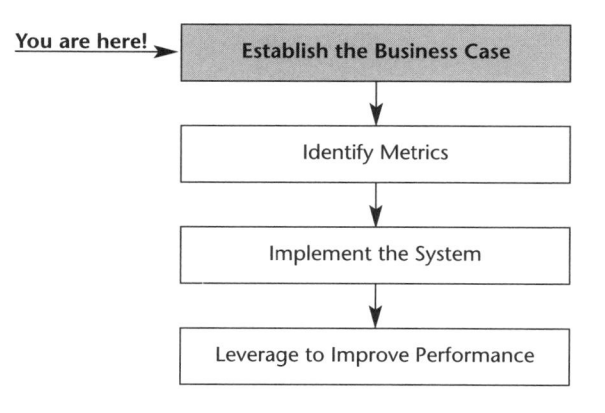

You are here! → Establish the Business Case

↓

Identify Metrics

↓

Implement the System

↓

Leverage to Improve Performance

show the value that a measurement system adds to the organization. We will discuss each later in the chapter to help you understand and complete them.

1. Develop a business case that involves assessing organizational initiatives, determining priorities for the initiatives, identifying performance interventions that address those initiatives, and selecting key indicators that measure success of the initiatives.
2. Create a strategic measurement council or task force that will set the direction and vision for the performance measurement system in the organization.
3. Develop a communication and marketing plan that will be used to sustain commitment and accountability of everyone in the organization to the performance measurement system.
4. Integrate the performance measurement system with other business processes.

Key Organizational Initiatives

A key component of any performance measurement system is identifying your organization's strategic goals, prioritizing them, selecting the right strategies and tactics to accomplish these goals, and determining performance measures that will reflect success. To collect data, you can conduct focus groups, hold one-on-one interviews, or send surveys to your executives and management team. Gather data from a variety of management perspectives—from top, middle, and first-line management—to ensure a direct alignment of business goals throughout the organization.

Some topics that must be covered in your interviews, focus groups, or surveys for the best possible results are described below.

Your Organization's Goals, Initiatives, and Key Priorities

Every department in your organization should be able to tell you about your organization's key initiatives and priorities for the future. Be it HR, training, finance, legal, manufacturing, or sales, you will have the best chance for success if all are aligned with the same priorities. Some possible organizational goals include the following:

- Increase units sold (volume)
- Improve customer service (or increase customer satisfaction)
- Increase market share
- Improve employee productivity

- Increase operational efficiency
- Improve product and service quality

Once the goals have been identified, help your organization to prioritize them according to degree of importance.

Identify Performance Gaps

Determine the difference between what is and what is wanted. In what specific areas do the business initiatives that have been identified fail to meet expectations? Where are the biggest gaps in processes, systems, communication, feedback, information, work environment, employee knowledge, and skills? For example, if your goal is to increase market share by 15 percent, what do sales, marketing, customer service, engineering, and other areas need to do to accomplish this? Here are some examples of questions you might ask to increase market share in the sales department of your organization:

- *Account Management Process.* Do you have a system for gathering information from your key customer accounts so that you can increase the value of these accounts?
- *Hiring and Recruiting.* Will you need to hire new sales representatives to handle increased demand?
- *Training.* Do your current sales employees have the knowledge and skills to grow and develop existing accounts?
- *Benefits and Compensation.* Are your sales executives rewarded for developing, retaining, and acquiring new accounts?
- *Job Process Tools.* Do your marketing and sales operations teams provide tools to make your salesforce more effective?

Once you have identified the performance gaps, you and your organization will have a better sense of what it takes to increase market share.

Address Causes of Performance Gaps

The next step is to identify specific causes and then to determine strategies for dealing with the gaps. Some examples of strategies and interventions that could be used to address causes of poor performance include training, education, process improvement, ergonomics, communication and feedback, coaching, reward systems, hiring and recruiting, and other change management programs. Work closely with the different business groups (for example, corporate communications, training, human resources, quality or process improvement group, business operations, or line management) so you can help them identify specific strategies that can be implemented.

For example, a high-tech sales organization we worked with implemented a selling course in its small customer group because our analysis showed that sales employees lacked the skills to qualify a customer prospect, position a company product that matched customer needs, manage objections that customers presented, and close a sale. In addition, the employees were not following a systematic, customer-focused, and consultative process. The objectives of the selling course were both to improve selling skills and to institute a sales process that focused on the customer. A return-on-investment study that we completed for 101 sales representatives who attended the training showed that their weekly profit margin increased by 10 percent, compared with a similar group of sales employees who had not yet attended the training. Clearly, there were multiple factors that led to an improvement, but identifying the right gaps will always lead to performance improvement.

Identify Barriers or Obstacles

Many obstacles can make accomplishing your goals difficult. If you can identify them, you can implement the proper strategies to overcome them. Otherwise, the performance desired will not be achieved. For example, you will not be able to implement a coaching program to motivate sales employees if first-line managers do not see its value and do not support it. In this case, you will have to involve top management in "selling" the coaching program. Another obstacle might be lack of hardware infrastructure and support. In this case, if you wanted to implement a new account management tool for account executives, you would need support from your operations and information systems or technology groups.

Identify Performance Measures

Find measures that will show that goals were accomplished. During your interviews, focus groups, or surveys with executives and top management, collect data on the measures that they use to define business success. If you use measures that your business clients do not value, then your measurement system will not work. For example, if you want to "increase market share," you must specifically identify the metric that measures market share—as defined by your business clients. Does market share mean volume or units sold, sales revenue or profit margin? Also be specific about the particular product line(s) being examined and the measures you will use.

Chapter Four describes the process of identifying the right measures and how to help your business clients agree to use these measures. For now, you can use

Tool 1 to incorporate performance measurement into your strategic planning process.

Here is an example of the results we obtained from using Tool 1 in one of the organizations that we have worked with.

1. *Prioritized business goals and percentage of responses*
   - Increase sales, market share, mix, average selling price, profit margin, product penetration, attach rate, and units—88 percent
   - Improve customer experience (total, internal, and external)—54 percent
   - Reduce cost and operating expenses to improve profitability—37 percent
   - Increase employee productivity (close rate, abandonment rate, performance)—33 percent
   - Maintain growth, increase Internet sales—28 percent
2. *Performance intervention priorities*
   - Sales and marketing, emphasis on selling servers, storage, service, closing and up-selling skills, synergistic competency-based sales, and marketing programs
   - Customer experience/process improvement initiatives
   - Competency-based solutions
   - Leadership/management development and professional skills, such as consulting, communication, teamwork, relationship building, creative thinking, time and project management
3. *Challenges and barriers to implementing initiatives*
   - Time and resources
   - System/structural improvement
   - Management coaching
   - Unclear expectations
   - Too much or lack of information
   - Management support, inconsistency in policy and management directives
   - IS/IT
4. *Key metrics for determining success of initiatives*
   - Sales: goal/quota attainment, product mix, market share, sales revenues, units sold, leasing penetration, demand units, account penetration rate, number of new accounts, up-sell metrics, product growth rates
   - Finance: revenue margin, average revenue per unit, average margin per unit, reduction in costs, adherence to budget, operating income
   - Performance/productivity: conversion rate, error rate, call abandonment rate, performance plans, number of committed customers, goal achievement, project dates/completion, efficiency, orders per hour rate, downtime reduction, same day entry percentage, factory shutdowns, output, close rate, attach rate, cycle time

TOOL 1

PERFORMANCE MEASUREMENT STRATEGIC PLANNING

What It's About

This is a tool that you can use to complete the steps involved in incorporating performance measurement into your organization's strategic planning process. You can use this as a framework for your management survey or as an interview template.

Purpose of Tool

1. Ensures that performance improvement efforts are directly linked with business priorities/initiatives.

2. Identifies relevant key success indicators for improving organizational and individual performance.

How to Customize

1. Personalize instructions and complete appropriate contact information for your audience.

2. Place company logo if used as a survey.

3. Change examples for each question to make sure they are relevant to your organization. The purpose of providing examples is to enhance understanding by your survey respondents, not to lead them to specific answers. Be specific about your sample metrics because sales organizations typically use different metrics and formulas for calculating profit margin or revenues.

4. Administer survey either through e-mail, regular intra-office mail, or any other convenient data collection method. You should know what works best for your organization. If used as an interview template, reproduce copies so the tool serves as a guide for each interview you conduct.

Instructions: Company ABCD is partnering with you to identify initiatives that will help you meet your business needs. Answer the following questions as clearly and honestly as you can. Your input is a critical part of our business planning process. Please complete this form by dd/mm/yyyy. If you have any questions, contact XXXXXXX at ######.

1. Prioritize your key business initiatives/issues/goals for next year. (Examples include increase product units sold, increase product market share, improve customer service, improve employee productivity)

2. What does the organization need to do in order to achieve these business goals? (Examples include implementing new technology, training, hiring new employees, developing new reward systems, improving physical workspace)

3. Please prioritize the above solutions in order of perceived importance.

4. What challenges/barriers will make accomplishment of these goals more difficult? (Examples include lack of employee skills, inefficient systems/processes, organizational culture)

5. What measures will you use to determine whether the business initiatives you identified in #1 are achieved? (Examples are sales revenues, volume of units sold, profit margin, number of customer complaints, cycle time, number of projects completed on time and on budget)

Integrating Performance Measurement with Existing Planning Processes

When building your business case for a performance measurement system, incorporate the following ideas so that management will see that measurement data already exists and/or how a performance measurement system can enhance planning processes that already exist. Position this in terms of how you can integrate your system into existing systems, not as a stand-alone activity.

By incorporating performance measurement into regular business activities, employees and managers can clearly see that it fits into the company structure. This will also increase the probability that management will buy into your process, because it does not take a lot of additional work. It is usually easy to piggyback data gathering onto regular duties in such a way that it adds very little work. Here are some examples of existing processes that you can leverage so that you can generate the data that you need.

The Strategic Business Planning Process

If you belong to a large organization, chances are you have a strategic business planning process in place. If so, you can add value to this process by influencing your management and executive team to incorporate outcomes such as key initiatives, priorities, and performance measures in the strategic plan. If you belong to a small organization or do not have a strategic planning process in place, then make sure you develop a simple mechanism for assessing your organization's plans, priorities, and metrics.

In a computer sales organization such as IBM, Compaq, or Dell, sales and financial measures drive the strategic planning process. Through a comprehensive analysis of the competition, industry trends, and the challenges of a high-tech environment, executives determine annual and quarterly goals. These overarching goals are then cascaded into objectives for individual business units and segments. These objectives then drive the priorities and strategic initiatives for each business unit or segment. The strategic planning process has built-in performance indicators that can serve as your framework for the company's or unit's performance measurement system.

In nonprofit organizations, there are sessions at least once a year to identify targets and priorities. If you are not involved in the process, find out who is in charge of the planning for these meetings and provide recommendations on how to incorporate measures in the planning document.

Financial and Budget Planning

Performance measurement planning should tie directly to your organization's financial and budget planning cycle. It is appropriate to start measurement planning at the beginning of this cycle, when your business identifies priorities and strategies and allocates resources. At this time the previous year's performance is examined. Also, you can provide management with specific information, such as market trends and customer preferences, to help them assess the competition.

Existing Planning Processes

Make use of existing human resource planning processes, such as head count resource planning, succession planning, and high potential planning. You can eliminate duplication of effort, as well as leverage data that are common to these processes. For example, training and development plans should be based on the same set of competencies that are used for recruitment and selection, performance planning, and development of high potential employees.

Other regular activities that generate measurement reporting data include quality control, risk management, engineering, accounting, payroll, and procurement.

Prioritize Interventions Based on Initiatives

After determining your organization's key initiatives, the next step is to prioritize the activities you have generated from using Tool 1 and to address the causes of any performance gaps in your organization. What are some of the factors to consider when prioritizing these activities? What key business indicators should you use to prioritize objectively?

Because change of any kind usually costs money, the return on investment (ROI) must be weighed against the long-term prosperity of the organization. A multi-million dollar supercomputer might speed up an operation immeasurably, but if your gross revenues are only a few hundred thousand per year, it's not worth the expense. On the other hand, if the computer will mean that you can now bid on larger projects and increase your revenues by several million dollars per year, then it may be worth the investment.

Here are both a process and a tool to determine your priorities. The process guarantees that the business impact of potential interventions will be considered and identified up-front. The process also forces you to think about specific measures that link your interventions with the goals of the organization. The process consists of three basic steps:

1. Determine the finance/cost/productivity/quality implications of each of the interventions you have identified. Calculate the potential benefits of each intervention in terms of finance metrics, such as cost, scrap rate, and warranty claims; then estimate the total cost of implementing each intervention.
2. Calculate potential return on investment (ROI). Calculate the potential ROI of each intervention by dividing the potential benefits by its estimated cost.
3. Compare ROI values and prioritize. You can next compare the ROIs you have calculated and prioritize your interventions by which will provide the biggest bang for your buck. Tool 2 provides you with a template for working through this prioritization process.

Here is an example of how we have used this tool for the selling course in the small business group in a high-tech sales organization.

This was a selling skills course, and the management team saw two key benefits for implementing the training program: (1) to improve profit margin for each system that sales representatives sold and (2) to increase close rate by having employees follow a systematic, customer-focused sales process. Here's an illustration of the calculation of the first potential benefit, improving profit margin.

Step 1. To determine the desired profit margin, the sales management team looked at the sales information database and analyzed current and historical average margins for each sales representative in the division. Based on this analysis, the team decided to set a monthly profit margin improvement target of $12k per sales representative. This amounted to $144k in annual potential increase for the one hundred sales representatives. Because of the confidentiality of the data, we will not provide detailed computations for this example.

Step 2. The two-day training program cost $799 per sales representative, for a total cost of $79,900, including both development and delivery of the course, along with the travel costs of the trainer.

Thus, in Step 2 of the tool, the estimated benefit is [Benefit – Cost] = [$144k – $79.9k] = $64,100. The potential ROI for this training, using only one metric, profit margin, would be at least $64,100/$79,900 = 0.80 or 80 percent.

Step 3. To obtain actual sales data, we used the company's sales information database system, which is the official source for sales metrics in the organization. We

TOOL 2
COST-BENEFIT ANALYSIS SPREADSHEET

What It's About

This is a tool that you can use to identify and prioritize performance improvement strategies and initiatives. It uses business criteria such as cost, quality, customer satisfaction, productivity, and sales for determining priorities.

Purpose of the Tool

1. Calculate return on investment of selected business strategies to assess their viability and feasibility.

2. Identify ranked order of priorities based on ROI calculations for each strategy.

How to Customize

1. The worksheet clearly describes the three basic steps needed to complete it. Personalize the specific metrics for each business criteria—cost, quality, customer satisfaction, productivity, and sales— so that it is relevant to your organization.

2. Collect data by working closely with the different departments or work groups that track metrics and generate reports.

3. Present your calculation results to the group that will make the decision on the strategies and actions that will be implemented. Develop a PowerPoint® presentation on your results, if appropriate.

TOOL 2 (Continued)

Project Name: _____

Worksheet completed by: _____ Date: _____

	STEP 1			STEP 3
	Do cost-benefit during front-end needs analysis and before funding cycle			Do ROI after intervention has been implemented
Intervention Benefit	**Current Data**	**Goal**	**Estimated Benefit**	**Actual Benefit**
Include all that apply:				
(Cheaper) Cost Data	$ _____	_____	$ _____	_____
(Faster) Time Data	$ _____	_____	$ _____	_____
(Better) Quality Data	$ _____	_____	$ _____	_____
Market Value (Stock Price & P/E Ratio)	$ _____	_____	$ _____	_____
Customer Satisfaction Data	$ _____	_____	$ _____	_____
(Grow Business) Sales Data	$ _____	_____	$ _____	_____
Estimate Percentage Impact of Intervention			_____%	_____
Estimated Dollar Benefit			#VALUE!	0

Attach documentation on data sources used to calculate
benefit and determine percentage impact.

STEP 2

Intervention Cost	**Estimated Cost**	**Actual Cost**
Development Costs	_____	_____
Delivery Costs	_____	_____
Estimated Cost =	0	0

Reference and attach spreadsheets used to calculate cost.

Estimated Benefit = [Benefit – Cost] =	0	0

Source: O'Brien, 1995.

used 101 employees who attended the telephone selling course during a three-week staggered schedule. As all employees cannot be taken off the sales queue at the same time, only 40 were scheduled to attend the training per week.

The actual results of the ROI study for 101 sales representatives yielded an average profit margin increase of 10 percent, resulting in annual benefits of $279k on this metric alone. With the total training expenses totalling $79,900, the actual benefits to the company from this metric alone is [$279k – 79.9k] or $199,100. The ROI for this training is $199,100/79,900 = 2.49 or 249 percent. This figure does not include the benefits in terms of close rate, which improved by 15 percent after the course for the same 101 employees. Other intangible benefits, such as improved customer satisfaction and improved efficiency, are also not quantified but contributed to improved performance by each sales representative.

Figure 3.1 illustrates how Tool 2 was used to complete the ROI study in the example above.

Other Priority Factors to Consider

It is important that you consider other factors aside from ROI when determining strategies and intervention priorities. The cost-linkage-infrastructure-visibility-effect (CLIVE) criteria explained below can be of help in prioritizing your initiatives:

C—Cost

The more costly the intervention, the more potential benefit you should be able to generate from it. For example, implementing new technology almost always requires high initial investment costs, and those involved usually have a comprehensive cost-benefit document showing the business impact of the project. It makes plain business sense to do this. Whenever we implement new performance technologies (such as a robust training registration system) in the sales organizations we work with, we have to conduct a thorough cost-benefit analysis to show how the project can improve operational efficiency, increase record-keeping effectiveness, and improve data accuracy.

L—Linkage

The more your intervention is linked to a key business initiative, the higher priority it should be. For example, if your organization wants to increase employee productivity as a top priority, but it does not have efficient and effective systems to

FIGURE 3.1. SAMPLE ROI ANALYSIS

Project Name: *Telephone Selling Course*
Worksheet completed by: *Ferdinand Tesoro*

	STEP 1 Do cost-benefit during front-end needs analysis and before funding cycle			**STEP 3** Do ROI after intervention has been implemented
Intervention Benefit	**Current Data**	**Goal**	**Estimated Benefit**	**Actual Benefit**
Include all that apply:				
(Cheaper) Cost Data	$ _____	_____	$ _____	_____
(Faster) Time Data	$ _____	_____	$ _____	_____
(Better) Quality Data	$ _____	_____	$ _____	_____
Market Value (Stock Price & P/E Ratio)	$ _____	_____	$ _____	_____
Customer Satisfaction Data	$ _____	_____	$ _____	_____
(Grow Business) Sales Data	$ _____	_____	$ 144,000	$ 144,000

Estimate Percentage Impact of Intervention	% 100%	10%
Estimated Dollar Benefit	$144,000	$279,000

Attach documentation on data sources used to calculate benefit and determine percentage impact.

STEP 2

Intervention Cost	**Estimated Cost**	**Actual Cost**
Development Costs	$79,000 (100 reps)	_____
Delivery Costs		
Estimated Cost =	$79,900	$79,900 (100 reps)

Reference and attach spreadsheets used to calculate cost.

Estimated Benefit = [Benefit – Cost] =	$64,100	$199,100

ROI = 64,100/79,900 = 0.8 or 80%   ROI = 199,100/79,900 = 2.5 or 250

Source: O'Brien, 1995.

support employees, then putting in new efficient systems should be a top priority. When we completed the first ROI study in one of the companies we consulted with, we chose a sales negotiation training program that was directly aligned with the company's sales revenue improvement goals. As a result, we had buy-in at the start to conduct the study, and we had a lot of existing data that were accessible.

I—Infrastructure

If your organization has well-established infrastructures for implementing an intervention, the higher its priority should be. Select interventions that have high probabilities of success. The infrastructure also determines your organization's degree of readiness for implementing the intervention.

As mentioned earlier, we had access to various sales data so it was relatively easy to complete the ROI study. The strong sales system and operational structure in the company allowed us easy access to the measurement data we needed.

V—Visibility

Also give high priority to interventions that can provide visibility to help your credibility within your organization. If you are in a sales-driven organization, activities that will enhance your visibility are those directly related to improving sales performance. Examples of these are customer-focused sales training, incentive systems for sales employees, and sales tools.

The opportunity/account management program at one of the manufacturing organizations we were involved with was implemented globally and at all levels in the organization—from regional sales managers and directors to account executives and sales representatives. It was a required course for all sales teams in the organization. Because of this, we conducted an ROI performance measurement study to show the value of accounts won and developed as a result of the training. The program required sales teams to develop a comprehensive sales plan for a live opportunity during the training, and a follow-up study was conducted after the training to determine whether these accounts were won or lost.

E—Effect

Deliver interventions that will have the most positive impact in your business. Interventions that address the biggest performance gaps will have the greatest impact. For example, if you want to increase market share by 10 percent, prioritize interventions that will help you get there, such as hiring new account executives, rolling out an intensive marketing campaign, and diversifying your product lines. Another example is the telephone selling course we implemented. It was clear at the start that this program would have a tremendous impact on salesforce performance because of the lack of a consistent sales process and the poor selling skills of the target audience.

Establishing a Strategic Council

It is imperative that line management be involved in key decisions concerning your organization. Along with performance consultants and HRD practitioners, they have to take ownership of the performance measurement process. One way of getting them involved is by forming a strategic council for performance measurement. The council can set the direction and tone for performance measurement for the rest of your organization.

Ideally, if you do not have a strategic measurement council in place in your organization, you should form one during the time that the business goals and priorities are being determined. If your organization does have a strategic business planning process, then you can use the team that develops the business plan as your measurement council. Use a cross-functional council so you can reach out to the entire organization as much as possible.

Advisory councils should be managed by an executive with the authority to implement initiatives or by someone whose recommendations carry real weight with management. Otherwise, the effort is an exercise in futility. The council should, at a minimum, possess the following characteristics:

- A clear understanding of goals and objectives, and a focus on the organization's key initiatives;
- Members with the desire to achieve the objectives, not just a willingness to attend;
- Members with clearly defined roles, responsibilities, and expectations; and
- Members who are actually involved in projects and initiatives and have a vested interest in their success.

The focus of the council should be on accomplishment, that is, on devising strategies to improve business performance, implementing remedial actions to correct or improve functional performance, and monitoring outcomes. The council must encourage and maintain an effective communication process. This is a key ingredient to its success. Published minutes of council meetings, details of action items and assignments, and explanations of key milestones are critical to maintaining the council's momentum.

So who should be in this council? What should be the responsibilities of this group? What are your operational guidelines? How can you keep it going? Tool 3 provides a template for answering these questions.

To address global education and performance improvement issues in one of the sales organizations we worked with, global sales, manufacturing, and management councils were formed to set the strategic direction for learning and education. The councils had executive sponsors or deans, along with boards that represented a cross-section of the organization, including training managers of the different regions. The councils met twice a year to coincide with the semi-annual global training executives' meeting. During these meetings, strategic priorities and action items were identified. Follow-up work for the councils was conducted through conference calls, e-mail, and other distance learning technologies.

Writing Your Business Case

Now that you have determined the key organizational initiatives, prioritized interventions, and formed a management council, you are ready to build your business case for implementing a global performance measurement system. What should be the key components you present in your business case? Use Tool 4 as a guide for presenting the value added from a performance measurement system.

A performance measurement system can be implemented at various levels of the organization. A system can involve the entire organization, the different business units, departments, or business groups, or individual employees. It is important that there be alignment among all of these levels of performance measurement systems. For example, there must be a clear link between overall goals and individual goals. When we logged on to our network in the sales organization we worked with, we immediately saw the status of global customer service metrics, a set of measures on how the organization was doing on customer satisfaction measures globally. By having information on how the company was performing globally, individual contributors and managers could identify measures that they could impact to improve the company's performance.

Once you have the business case, you have a consistent message to communicate to everyone in your organization regarding the value and potential business impact of performance measurement. Be patient and do not expect executives to accept this process right away. You first have to establish your credibility and build trust with your business clients. Make sure you understand their business and speak the language of the business executives. For example, speak about reducing costs, increasing sales, increasing efficiency, and improving employee productivity.

TOOL 3

STRATEGIC COUNCIL FOR PERFORMANCE MEASUREMENT

What It's About

A strategic council for performance measurement is essential if you want your organization to be directly involved in your performance measurement process. It provides an opportunity for your business clients to set the strategic direction for performance measurement in their organization. This tool provides you with some guidelines for setting up this council.

Purpose of Tool

1. Provide specific guidelines on how to set up, manage, and implement a strategic council for performance measurement.

How to Customize

1. Use the tool as a framework for organizing your own council. Select council members who can best carry out the responsibilities described in the tool.

2. As much as possible, let your business clients own the performance measurement process. Your major responsibilities are facilitating group discussions, developing structured guidelines, and communicating expectations and results.

3. You can successfully operate this "virtual" council as long as you have a good communication process in place for getting feedback, generating recommendations, and making decisions.

4. This council does not have to be a stand-alone council. For example, if a cross-functional team has been assigned by top executives to come up with a strategy for increasing customer satisfaction, you can leverage this team by influencing the right people to build in performance measures as they develop strategies and tactics for addressing this business problem.

Each organizational segment (e.g., Americas, Asia, South America, Europe) and each corporate function (e.g., Engineering, Finance, Legal,

HR, Sales) should be represented in your strategic council. You may also decide that councils may exist at different levels—executive and senior management, first-line management, and employees. These councils are the principal structure for all decisions regarding the business plan, the execution of that plan, and the evaluation of results. Among the responsibilities of the councils are:

1. Approval of key initiatives and intervention priorities.

2. Budget approval for the cost implications of the implementation of initiatives.

3. Approval of performance metrics.

4. Monitoring of performance metrics.

5. Marketing and communication of performance measurement throughout the organization.

6. Ownership for measurement in the business/function.

These councils will be managed by an appropriate executive and typically are chaired by the head of the business or function. These councils will most often have a global mission, though they could be formed to address needs across regional groups.

Expectations for Strategic Council

The council for performance measurement should possess these characteristics:

1. An able and credible council chair. A leader, not just a "content expert." A high-level executive who is a strong advocate for performance measurement would make a good chair.

2. Clear objectives and a vision of what the council is to accomplish. The objectives should focus on the organization's key initiatives as identified in Step 1.

3. Membership of the council should be based on the objectives, not just willingness to attend. It is important that the diversity of perspectives and ideas be covered in the council.

4. Clearly defined roles, responsibilities, and expectations. It is important that this be communicated up-front to each council member.

TOOL 3 (Continued)

5. Involve council participants, not just people who attend the meetings. Involve them in projects, presentations, etc., when appropriate.

6. Determine appropriate frequency and length of meetings. When holding meetings, make sure you have specific objectives that you want to accomplish. Also, focus your meetings on deliverables and outcomes to sustain your performance measurement process.

7. Clearly determine in advance how the council can deliver against the personal objectives of the participants. It is key that council goals and member interests be aligned so that members can benefit from the measurement process as well.

8. A robust communication process is a key ingredient to the success of the council. Council meeting minutes, action items, and key milestones are critical to maintaining the council's continuity and momentum.

9. Determine when the work of the council will be completed and identify major milestones along the way so each member feels a sense of accomplishment and closure.

TOOL 4

ESTABLISHING YOUR BUSINESS CASE

What It's About

This tool is a simple template that establishes a simple, business-based justification for your performance measurement system. It addresses questions on what is it, what's-in-it-for-me, how will we do this, when will this happen, who will be involved, and what we need from you to make performance measurement happen.

Purpose of Tool

1. Provides a template that includes the basic components of the business case you need for any performance improvement project you are proposing.

2. Ensures that any performance improvement strategy is directly aligned with the needs of the business.

How to Customize

1. Make sure you customize this tool for your company by using culture-specific and goal-driven language. This is especially needed when you identify "what's-in-it-for-them." Make an effort to understand the "hot buttons" of each key business executive and decision maker. This will be the only way you can get their attention and eventual buy-in.

2. Use this tool as your selling document. You can place the content in a PowerPoint® presentation or in whatever format is appropriate in your organization. You can also use this as your opening remarks for the kickoff meeting of your strategic council.

What is it?

Develop a short description of your performance measurement system here. It is important that this description be succint, simple, and comprehensive. This is your 60-second elevator presentation.

TOOL 4 (Continued)

What's in it for you?

Write the benefits of performance measurement to your business. What can they derive from having a measurement system?

What's the roll-out timeline?

List your timeline here with major milestones. If possible, divide your implementation into phases so that they are easy to manage and track. It is also important that throughout your project you provide a sense of successful accomplishment to your business.

Phase 1

Phase 2

Phase 3

What we need from you to make this happen

Describe specific decisions that you need your business advisory councils to decide on. Also, be particular about the actions you need them to take to support the measurement process.

Who is on the project team?

Describe your project team here, including your champion and sponsors. Make sure you also include your IT department consultants if the project involves technology.

Developing a Communication and Marketing Plan

Part of your business case should be a communication and marketing plan that outlines who your target audience is, what information needs to be sent to that audience, how it should be sent, and when the appropriate time is to send it. This plan is particularly critical if you want an effective "virtual" council. The single biggest reason for success (or failure) of any project is the level of communication among members of a cross-functional, enterprise-wide project team.

Tool 5 can be customized as you develop your communication and marketing plan.

Key success factors for implementing performance measurement systems include management involvement and clear communication of measurement results throughout the organization. It is important that a communication and marketing plan be identified up-front for your measurement efforts.

◆ ◆ ◆

Key Summary Points

The following are the key points covered in this chapter.

1. To establish a solid business case for performance measurement, first identify your organization's key priorities, initiatives, and goals. Once these are determined, measure your performance against accomplishment of these goals.
2. To determine the return on investment (ROI) of any intervention, divide the total cost of implementing the intervention by its benefits (in terms of productivity, revenue, cost savings, and so forth).
3. Other factors should also be considered when determining organizational priorities, such as impact on business initiatives, infrastructure systems, visibility, and direct links between your intervention and business goals.
4. It is important that a communication and marketing plan be developed for performance measurement in order to solicit commitment from top management. This is also key to gaining line managers' ownership of the performance measurement process.

TOOL 5
COMMUNICATION AND MARKETING PLAN

What It's About

The following tool generates commitment and buy-in to your performance measurement system by providing a structured, business-focused communication and marketing plan. This has to be totally integrated in the process for your system to be successful. Even if you are doing the right things for the business, you cannot assume that the messages your measurement brings reach the audience that can most benefit from them. You have to deliver the right metrics and the right analysis to the right people at the right time.

Purpose of Tool

1. Describes a time-based communication and marketing strategy that gets the right messages to measurement audiences.

2. Provides a concrete framework for keeping focus on the needs of the business by communicating what, when, to whom, and how of performance measurement.

How to Customize

1. You need to customize the content of this tool so it specifically addresses the communication issues in your company. Leverage existing systems such as e-mail, team meetings, and one-on-one sessions in communicating status and results of your performance measurement system.

2. When communicating measurement results, make sure you consider the target audience for the message. For example, your top executives don't have time to read a ten-page plan, so you need to develop a half-page executive summary to communicate key results to them. Choose the appropriate medium for communicating the message by examining what each of your audiences is most comfortable with. Executives may prefer one-on-one, ten-minute sessions, whereas e-mail may work for the majority of your business clients.

When to Communicate	What to Communicate	Where to Send Message	How to Send Message
Establishing the business case—Step 1	Business Case— What is it? What's the business value? What's in it for me? What do you need to do to make this happen?		
Identifying the right metrics— Step 2	List of metrics— organization, segment, department, and individual metrics		
Implementing the system— Step 3	Accomplishments, timeline for major milestones, project status, lessons learned		
Leveraging to improve performance— Step 4	Results, reports, comparative analysis, trends, measurement scorecard		

APPLICATION EXERCISE: CASE STUDY, CHAPTER THREE

ESTABLISHING THE BUSINESS CASE FOR PERFORMANCE MEASUREMENT AT FJT TECH

Discussion: Questions and Answers

You have won the support of the senior vice president of sales to proceed with making a presentation to senior management on the implementation of a global performance measurement system (GPMS) for FJT Tech. Using the knowledge you have learned in this chapter, here are some questions and answers that will help you establish the business case for performance measurement at FJT Tech:

1. What should be the immediate next steps that you take to address FJT Tech's business problem?

   In FJT Tech, you were lucky enough to have a cross-functional team already formed. In other situations, you may not have such a task force from which you can get information and support. In these situations, you will need to find an existing business council, champion, or any other cross-functional executive team that you can use as your sponsor for the GPMS.

   You can leverage the cross-functional task force that was formed to address the business problem by asking the team the following key questions. You will use the information here in the business case that you will present to senior management. These questions can be found in Tool 1, Identifying Strategic Goals and Initiatives.

   - What are FJT Tech's business goals and initiatives that respond to competitor actions?

   - What is the priority of these goals according to degree of importance and urgency?

   - To accomplish these goals, what performance needs to happen? What do the organization and its employees need to do to achieve the desired prioritized goals? In which areas can improving performance make the greatest impact? For example, find a new software for product designers that can accelerate new product design and development or embark on an intensive advertising plan to sustain shareholder and market credibility.

- To address these performance gaps, what specific interventions and programs need to be implemented at FJT Tech? Do these initiatives really focus on the root causes of performance gaps?

- What specific indicators could signify that these interventions are successful? How will you know that you have accomplished your prioritized business goals?

2. How will you collect data on FJT Tech's short-and long-term goals and priorities?

   Again, it will be valuable if you use the cross-functional task force to come up with the plan for this. Along with the data generated by the task force, what you can suggest is that each member talk with selected key executives in their functional areas using the same questions listed above. It will also be helpful to survey the pulse of the first-line and second-line managers to get their input on what the company should be doing to move forward. We suggest that this survey be done electronically through e-mail or any other survey technology so that you get as much feedback as possible. If technology use is not possible, then you can use hard copy or other means of communication that is convenient for everybody. Finally, the employees' views should also be taken into consideration. Surveying a sample of employees from each functional area or attending sales team meetings can be used here. Use the questions in Tool 1 in Chapter 3.

   It also seems that the company has to do a lot of engineering and market research so they can be more proactive in the future in coming up with product design and marketing strategies. Some questions you might ask to surface these issues include:

   - What are customers' requirements and preferences for features in wireless phones?

   - How can FJT Tech meet future customer requirements and needs?

   - Because FJT Tech's mission is to provide state-of-the-art products, what existing and future technologies can be used to keep the company on the cutting edge for wireless phone products?

3. What will you do once you gather the data?

   All of this information must be collated so that the cross-functional task force can analyze it and come up with a comprehensive business plan. To arrive at the priorities, use Tool 2, the Cost-Benefit Analysis Worksheet. Each of the ROI calculations in this situation is simplified for illustration purposes. The actual computations of benefits, cost, and ROI can be complex, depending on the project you are working on. In the FJT Tech case, the top four priorities, based on ROI rank from highest to lowest, can be:

- Immediately slash prices of the current product, although this will result in reduced revenues. Although this reduces revenues for FJT Tech in the short-term, it can prevent huge potential loss in market share until the new revolutionary product is introduced. Using the three-step process in Tool 2, the following ROI was computed:

  Step 1: To calculate benefits in terms of reduction in potential long-term losses to the company, it is estimated that slashing prices will save the company around $30M loss due to poor sales. The short-term cost (revenue loss) due to slashing of these prices will be, say about $2M. Thus, ROI for this option = $30M/$2M = 15 or 1,500 percent. Because of this high potential ROI value, this option is top priority.

- Invest $2M to speed up introduction of the next-generation wireless digital phone that has additional features but weighs less. Although the cost for introducing this new product is high, customer research says that this revolutionary product will have immediate impact on market share and revenues. Customers' top requirements include use of cutting-edge technologies and "lighter" phones. Below is how the ROI process was used for this option:

  Step 1: The benefit to FJT Tech of this option will be the potential increase in revenue and market share for this product once it is introduced. You can ask product forecasters to determine the initial projections for number of units sold, profit margin, and total sales revenues. Assume that you will have the potential of increasing revenues by about $8M during the first year.

  Step 2: The cost to the company for this will be the $2M for product design and development.

  Step 3: ROI = Benefits/Cost = $8M/$2M = 4 or 400 percent. This option has the second highest ROI so this will be the second priority for this project.

- Introduce an advertising campaign to sustain market credibility. Estimated additional advertising cost for this effort is $1M. This strategy is important in preventing loss of large corporate accounts and winning new ones. The return-on-investment for this strategy or the expense for this campaign is expected to be recoverable within one year due to loss prevention and potential new accounts won. Here is how the ROI for this option was calculated:

Step 1: Benefits to the company = $2.5M additional revenues due to advertising campaign.

Step 2: Cost to the company = $1M.

Step 3: ROI = Benefits/Cost = $2.5M/$1M = 2.5 or 250 percent.

- Train sales people on new sales approach and features/benefits of the soon-to-be-released product. Estimated cost for implementing this solution is $75k. Providing this training intervention will increase selling skills of sales representatives, especially in the areas of qualifying customer needs, positioning the new product, and managing objections of customers. This can potentially increase revenues and close rates of sales representatives by 5 to 10 percent, and the $75k price tag can be recovered in one to two years. The ROI calculation for this initiative is shown below:

Step 1: Benefits to the company = 5 – 10 percent increase in sales employee revenues due to training = $100k per year.

Step 2: Cost to the company = Training development and delivery cost = $75k.

Step 3: ROI = Benefits/Cost = $100k/$75k = 1.33 or 133 percent.

4. What is an outline of the business case that you will present to senior management?

After you have completed these steps, use Tool 4, Establishing Your Business Case, as your guide in developing your "sales pitch" to the cross-functional task force on the value of performance measurement. Based on our experiences, a reasonable timeline for implementation at FJT Tech can be:

Phase 1: Establishing business case. About 2 weeks.

Phase 2: Identifying metrics. About 2 weeks.

Phase 3: Implementing the system, including pilot, revisions, and full rollout. About 6 weeks.

Phase 4: Leveraging results. After 10 weeks.

Completing the four phases in 10 weeks will be perfect timing, as the new product will be available in two to three months, and by this time you should really have a good ongoing performance tracking system in place.

Your project team here should include the entire cross-functional task force. Specific members who will have particular roles in implementing the system will be the vice president of finance, who will provide the cost reports; the senior sales vice president, who can help you with access to sales revenue, profit margin, and units sold data; the marketing VP, who can provide you with access to the advertising schedule; and the VP for engineering, who can give you inside information on the new product that is being designed and developed.

5. Who should you recommend as members of your strategic council for performance measurement in FJT Tech?

   It is clear that the current cross-functional team, which is developing the business plan for FJT Tech, is the best candidate for the strategic council. You have started to help the team own the process and this will surely enhance commitment and buy-in to the task at hand. Make sure that you use Tool 3 as a reference on how this measurement council can operate.

6. What are the key messages that you need to include in FJT Tech's communication and marketing plan? Who are the target audiences for these messages?

   Using Tool 5, a sample Communication and Marketing Plan is provided below for FJT Tech.

When to Communicate	What to Communicate	Where to Send Message	How to Send Message
Establishing the business case for measurement— Weeks 1–2	Business case that includes FJT Tech's 4 priorities—slash prices, build new product, advertise, and train sales employees. Show how the ROI for each option was selected so your audience realizes the benefits of each to the company.	Strategic council, all segments, departments, and corporate functions	One-on-one meetings, presentation to strategic council
Identifying the right metrics— Weeks 1–2	List of key metrics, including sales revenues, profit margin, units sold, advertising cost, new product design cost, and training cost	All segments, departments, executives, and managers	Written memo, e-mail message with follow-up in team meetings
Implementing the system— Starting Week 5	Deliver revenue reports showing product volume, revenue and margin trends, and when each option was implemented	Strategic council, all segments, departments, and corporate functions	E-mail messages, team meetings
Leveraging to improve performance— Starting Week 10	Follow-up report on how reports were used to reinforce training skills learned by sales employees, determine appropriate time for showing advertisements, and project revenues and volume sold based on current data trends	Strategic council, all segments, departments, and corporate functions	Ongoing web or online reports

CHAPTER FOUR

IDENTIFYING THE RIGHT PERFORMANCE METRICS

Now that you have made your business case to senior management and won approval to proceed with your performance improvement initiatives, it is time to identify the right performance metrics. Let's look at where we are on the model, first presented in Chapter Two.

This chapter gives you some simple frameworks for identifying the right performance metrics for your organization. Three basic criteria for determining what is appropriate for your team, department, or business unit will be discussed. Finally, a template for collecting baseline data and determining appropriate targets will be provided.

One of the biggest challenges in implementing a performance measurement system is knowing what to measure. Some organizations find it relatively easy to determine the appropriate measures to track, while others may have a more difficult time. The ease or difficulty of finding the appropriate metrics for

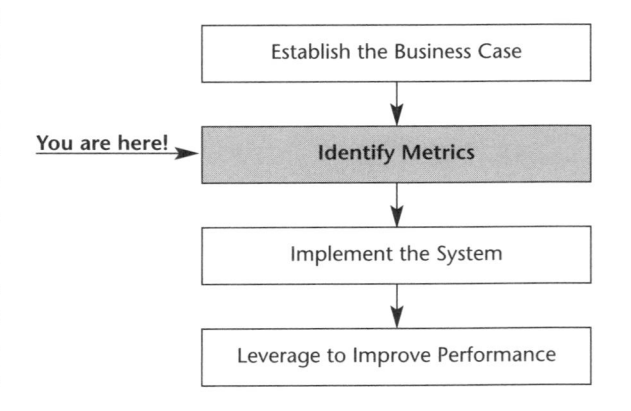

Establish the Business Case

You are here! → **Identify Metrics**

Implement the System

Leverage to Improve Performance

performance improvement depends on many factors, such as type of organization, nature of products and services delivered, type of customers, knowledge of the organization's strategic goals and priorities, maturity of internal systems, and availability of tangible data.

Manufacturing and industrial organizations may have a relatively easier time identifying metrics that reflect organizational performance than government agencies and nonprofit organizations. The fact that the first group has tangible products that they deliver to customers (that is, computers, airplanes, gasoline) makes it relatively easier for them to find performance metrics, compared to the service-oriented and nontangible products delivered by the others. Another difference is that the first group has a more well-defined customer set and corresponding needs, whereas the second group has a more generic audience. For example, a sales organization divides its market into segments such as consumers, small businesses, large corporate accounts, public and international, and enterprises for which it specifically customizes its products. This makes it easier for them to find the appropriate measures for success of each market segment. Clearly defined customer needs make it easy for the different units and departments to determine how they have performed in meeting these needs.

Organizations that have well-articulated and clearly communicated strategic goals also have a better chance of finding the right measures to track and manage their performance relative to these goals. This is even true for nonprofit organizations, which sets fund-raising revenue and percentage targets for the different organizations that support it. Organizations that have well-documented processes and systems also increase their likelihood of identifying the right measures, especially if benchmarking and feedback loops are built into these systems. Finally, organizations that provide access to business data, such as revenues, costs, or customer satisfaction, to the right people can effectively use these metrics to manage performance better.

What's the cost of not identifying the right measures? Take for example a large manufacturing organization of approximately 15,000 employees that did not track performance as a result of a changing business environment. Products were designed and manufactured to serve a limited client base. Even though the corporate strategic plan suggested expanding the client base, the manufacturing plant did not identify key measurable indicators, such as shifting to a broader client base, establishing customer quality indicators and needs, and adapting to new efficiency parameters. Because it did not shift its emphasis in response to critical customer needs, the plant began to lose its major client and was not able to expand into other customer markets. As a result, people were laid off, assembly lines were dismantled, and the organization took a huge loss—all as a result of not identifying and matching measurement tools to address the changing business environment.

Several years later, the organization went out of business. This company learned a hard lesson about the need to identify performance standards and measures, especially in a volatile business environment.

This chapter will provide you with the knowledge and tools to help you identify the right metrics to help your organization move forward.

Criteria for Identifying the Right Metrics

There are three basic criteria for identifying the right metrics to track and manage organizational and individual performance better. You must find measures that are:

- Credible, relevant, and valuable
- Widely used and based on standards
- Available and accessible

Let's discuss these criteria and why they are important, as well as the tools you need to ensure that your metrics follow these criteria.

Credible, Relevant, and Valuable

Use metrics that are credible, relevant, and valuable to the management team in your organization. Provide metrics to these people so that they can use them to run the business. How do you know which metrics are credible, relevant, and valuable to these key decision makers? Start with measures that are directly linked to the organization's goals and the cascading tactical strategies for the different departments. In a sales organization, for example, if a strategic goal is to increase market share by 15 percent, the executive team may assign specific targets for each customer group or segment. For example, the large corporate accounts group may have a greater target, say 20 percent, because of their greater potential to increase market share. The small business or home consumer group, on the other hand, may have a lower target of 10 percent. You can include tracking any change in the market share percentage and the cascading targets for each customer group or segment. Examples of what to track include sales revenues, unit volume, profit margin, and number of new accounts acquired.

You can also ask executives and managers what their performance objectives are for the year. This will surely attract their interest and attention because they have a vested interest in accomplishing their objectives. The metrics that executives value depend on what departments they run. If the goal is to "increase market share by 15 percent," as in the example, the executive in information technology will be interested in showing how the efficiency and effectiveness of information systems made sales employees more productive. An executive in the training organization may want to measure the impact of sales training on increased new accounts or revenue penetration, which may in turn lead to increase in market share. Table 4.1 illustrates this example.

The point is that the metrics for your performance measurement system should be tied directly to organizational and individual goals and objectives.

Tool 6 can be used to link your metrics to business goals. It provides a template and examples for identifying the appropriate metrics, given your organization's goals and objectives.

Widely Used and Based on Standards

The second criterion is to use metrics that are widely used and standard across almost all types of organizations. Using these generic metrics allows you to benchmark to determine how your organization is doing relative to the industry or the competition.

Professional organizations such as the American Society for Training and Development (ASTD) conduct benchmarking studies that compare quality, productivity, customer satisfaction, and business impact data among different types of organizations. Examples of metrics that are compared are investment as a percentage of payroll, training effectiveness, training impact, and types of training conducted.

TABLE 4.1. HOW COMPANY GOALS CASCADE TO DEPARTMENT METRICS

Company Goal	Department	Specific Targets	Metrics
Increase market share by 15%	IT	Reduce troubleshooting time for sales ordering software program issues	• Number of software problems addressed • Troubleshooting time per problem reported
Increase in new accounts won	Training	Increase product knowledge and positioning skills	• Number of new accounts won • Close rate (number won/ total number opportunities)

TOOL 6

LINKING METRICS WITH GOALS

What It's About

This tool provides a framework and process for directly linking performance improvement initiatives with your organization's business goals. It shows an example of a strategic goal for a particular department in an organization and the corresponding indicators that measure success for this goal.

Purpose of Tool

1. Ensures direct linkage between organization goals and key indicators that reflect success.

2. Identifies credible, relevant, and valuable metrics.

How to Customize

1. This tool is meant as a guide for you. To use it, identify the type of organization that is closely related to yours.

2. Identify one or more strategic goals that pertain to your organization or department.

3. Finally, select the metrics that are appropriate for the goals that you have identified.

4. Customize each of the metrics you selected for your organization. For example, defect rate can be modified to number of customer complaints relative to total number served. Here are some more examples:

   - *Customer Satisfaction Rating.* Percent of projects delivered according to customer specs, percent of customers whose expectations are met or exceeded.

   - *Business Impact Measure.* Dollars saved due to interventions, cost reduced as a result of introducing program, time savings due to use of online training versus classroom training.

   - *Productivity Measure.* Dollars generated per volunteer, number of projects completed per month, number of new accounts won by account executive, number of audits completed per week.

Example

Department	Strategic Goal	Business Metrics
Product Manufacturing	• Improve product quality	• Defect rate— number of complaints vs. number total customers served • Percent product according to specifications— percent products with deviations below 2-sigma • Return rate—number products returned vs. total sold or shipped • Customer satisfaction ratings—percent customers whose expectations were met or exceeded (i.e., at least 4.0 on a 5.0 scale)

Template

Department	Strategic Goal	Business Metrics
Sales		
Operations		
Engineering		
Manufacturing		
Finance		
Legal		
Human Resources		
Corporate Communications		
Information Technology		

Tool 7 is an example of a performance measurement scorecard that includes basic metrics for productivity, quality, customer satisfaction, and impact. It has been used by a variety of organizations in different industries. The actual metrics can vary for specific organizations and departments. Examples of metrics for a training department are given in the tool. Use this same framework for developing your own metrics for a specific department or work group.

Here is an example of how we used a quarterly performance scorecard in a very successful retail organization (25 percent increase in profits for four years in an industry that averages 10 percent growth). The articulation of strategic initiatives started with the chief executive and extended all the way through the organization. The chief executive made presentations on a quarterly basis. By using simple visual symbols, quarterly results were communicated to every employee. Each person knew how his or her contribution affected the bottom line. The company's performance plan reflected the three key metrics of their market—no more than 2 percent manufacturing waste, successful introduction of a minimum of five products, and less than 1 percent customer complaints. Organizations who can sustain high growth are good at taking their strategic points and drilling them down through individual performance plans. The simpler the message, the easier it is to follow and to come up with guidelines in order to accomplish desired results.

Available and Accessible

The third criterion is to use metrics that are available and accessible to you and your company. Do not reinvent the wheel. Use measures that are currently being tracked and reported by the various departments. For example, check with accounting or finance to see what weekly or monthly reports they generate. Or talk with your operations department to see what data they provide to sales management on a regular basis. Request that you be included on distribution lists so you have access to the information. You may also want to request that you have the spreadsheet version of a report so you can manipulate the data and do some analysis. Check with engineering, information technology, manufacturing, finance, legal, and human resources.

Tool 8 provides some initial steps to take to determine sources of metrics in your company. Sample metrics for each source are provided.

Framework for Collecting Metrics Data

After identifying the right performance metrics to track, you are well on your way to having a well-founded performance measurement system. The next steps are to generate baseline data and to identify targets for each of the metrics you have identified.

TOOL 7

PERFORMANCE MEASUREMENT SCORECARD

What It's About

This is a tool that provides a consistent, goal-centered framework for identifying appropriate standard measures for performance. It also gives examples of specific department metrics that represent each major category.

Purpose of Tool

1. Identifies standard categories for measuring performance.

2. Shows examples of specific department metrics under each major standard category.

How to Customize

1. Use the same standard categories described in the tool: quality, productivity, impact, and customer satisfaction.

2. Use the examples listed for each category to guide you in developing your own departmental metrics.

TOOL 7 (Continued)

Example

Business Driver	Key Measures	Metrics for Performance Consulting/Training Department
Productivity	• Units per unit time • Units per person • Dollars per unit	• Number of Web-based courses developed per year • Number of learning solutions designed and developed per instructional designer • Number of customers serviced by staff • Dollars generated per trainer/performance consultant • Average dollars per Web-based course
Quality	• Defects • Cycle time	• Average service time • Cycle time per solution • Cycle time per product
Customer Satisfaction	• Ratings	• Customer satisfaction index
Impact/ROI	• Time • Dollars • Intangibles	• Dollars and time saved due to process improvement • Incremental profit dollars due to better training • Number of processes defined or improved • Decrease in on-the-job accidents due to better safety programs
Business Initiative	• Integration • Efficiency • Financial stability	• Number and percentage of global solutions produced • Average cost per performance solution • Dollars generated from training tuition

Template

Business Driver	Key Measures	Metrics for Performance Consulting/Training Department
Productivity	• Units per unit time • Units per person • Dollars per unit	
Quality	• Defects • Cycle time	
Customer Satisfaction	• Ratings	
Impact/ROI	• Time • Dollars • Intangibles	
Business Initiative	• Integration • Efficiency • Financial stability	

TOOL 8

TYPES OF DEPARTMENT AND FUNCTIONAL METRICS

What It's About

This tool gives a comprehensive list of different types of department and functional metrics. These metrics are generic enough for any type of organization to use.

Purpose of Tool

1. Gives specific examples of metrics that can be used to measure performance.

2. Provides measures that represent different areas of the business.

How to Customize

1. Use this as a guide to determine metrics that are relevant to the different functional areas of the organization. For example, if you work in human resources, use the HR metrics to show the impact of your department on the organization. Analyze the column on strategic goals and identify those that pertain to your organization's priorities.

2. Customize each of the metrics you selected for your organization. For example, defect rate can be modified to number of customer complaints relative to total number served. Other examples of customized metrics are shown below:

   • *Customer Satisfaction Rating.* Percentage of projects delivered according to customer specs, percentage of customers whose expectations are met or exceeded by the service you provided.

   • *Business Impact Measure.* Dollars saved due to interventions, cost reduced as a result of introducing program, time savings due to use of online training versus classroom training.

   • *Productivity Measure.* Dollars generated per volunteer, number of projects completed per month, number of new accounts won by account executive, number of audits completed per week.

Example

Department/ Function	Sample Metrics	
Sales	• Total Sales Revenues • Percentage of Accounts Retained • Percentage of Accounts Grown (up-selling) • Number of Units Sold • Percentage of Increase in Market Share	• Percentage of Quotas Met or Exceeded • Average Selling Price • Manufacturer's Selling Price • Number of Recorded Customer Complaints • Profit Margin Per Unit Sold
Finance/ Accounting	• Return on Investment/Return on Investment Capital • Forecast of Product Cost Margin (FPC) • Net Revenue • Operating Income • Net Income • Earnings Per Share • Cash • Marketable Securities	• Accounts Receivable • Inventories • Total Assets • Total Liabilities • Accrued Debt • Accounts Payable • Stockholders' Equity • Days' Supply in Inventory
Customer Service	• Customer Satisfaction Index • Cost Per Customer Complaint • First Time First Fix Rate	• Number of Customer Complaints • Service Time Per Customer • Service Cost Per Customer
Legal	• Number of Liability Cases Filed • Number of Cases Settled • Dollar Value of Cases Successfully Defended	• Dollar Value of Cases Prevented Due to Clear Policies and Procedures
Manufacturing	• Units Produced • Tons Manufactured • Items Assembled • Items Sold	• Work Volume Backlog • Number of Units Shipped • Equipment Downtime

TOOL 7 (Continued)

Department/ Function	Sample Metrics	
Manufacturing (cont.)	• Forms Processed • Inventory Turnover Rate • Tasks Completed • Output per Hour • Order Response Time • Lost Time Days • Production Cost • Production Cost as Percentage of Total Cost	• Overtime • On Time Shipments • Time to Project Completion • Processing Time • Training Time • Repair Time • Work Stoppages
Quality/ Engineering Metrics	• Scrap Percentage • Rework Percentage • Reject Rate • Error Rate • Waste Percentage • Number of Shortages • Product Defects • Deviation from Standard • Product Failures • Inventory Adjustments • Number of Inventory Turns per Day	• Number of Accidents • Budget Variances • Unit Cost • Variable and Fixed Cost • Overhead Cost • Operating Cost • Number of Cost Reductions • Project Cost Savings • Accident Costs • Percent of Tasks Completed Properly • Number and Cost of Warranty Claims
Marketing	• Dollar Investments for Marketing • Documented Dollar Returns for Marketing Investment • Number of Marketing Plays Implemented	• Number and Percent of Customers Reached by Marketing Plays • Deviation Between Actual and Forecast Sales Revenues
Human Resources Management	• Absenteeism • Tardiness • Visits to the Dispensary • First Aid Treatments	• Litigation • Job Enlargement • Number of Employees in Company for More Than 10 Years

- Violations of Safety Rules
- Excessive Breaks
- Number of Grievances
- Number of Discrimination Charges
- Decisions Made
- Problems Solved
- Conflicts Resolved
- Grievances Addressed
- Counseling Problems Solved
- Discrimination Charges Resolved
- Frequency of Use of New Skills
- Number of Promotions

- Perceived Increase by Others
- Perceived Changes in Performance
- Employee Complaints
- Employee Turnover Rate
- Number of Pay Increases
- Number of Training Programs Attended
- Requests for Transfer
- Performance Appraisal Ratings
- Increase in Job Effectiveness
- Implementation of New Ideas
- Successful Completion of Projects
- Number of Suggestions Submitted
- Suggestions Implemented

Training and Education

- Number of Students, Training Classes, Total Hours, Total Tuition
- Percent of Total Training Classes Delivered by Region/Area
- Number and Percent of No-Shows (students who registered but did not show up)
- Percent of Target Audience Who Benefitted from Performance Intervention

- Actual vs. Forecast Utilization Rate on Program/Course Attendance
- Percent of Target Audience Who Completed Compliance Requirements
- Dollar Cost for No-Shows
- Average Investment Per Training Hour

Template

Department/ Function	Your Metrics
Sales	
Finance/Accounting	
Customer Service	
Legal	
Manufacturing	
Quality/Engineering Metrics	
Marketing	
Human Resource Management	
Training and Education	

Establish Baseline Data

Once you have singled out the key performance indicators, you need to collect baseline data on these metrics. This is important because the only way you can tell whether you are successful is to determine whether your numbers are better than your baseline data.

What baseline should you choose? As much as possible, use both historical and current data available for each metric. Never just use the most current information as a baseline. The risk is that recent information may not be truly reflective of past performance. For example, if your company's sales are seasonal, your baseline data would be too high if you gathered it during the peak times. On the other hand, collecting baseline data only during the slower period would give a false sense of sales growth. One way of addressing data fluctuation is to look at a longer time period (such as a year) and then identify any cyclical trends. In the computer industry, either yearly or quarterly data can be used for baseline purposes, comparing the current quarter either to the quarter just past or to the same quarter a year earlier.

In a customer service organization we worked with, baseline data were used in a variety of ways. The call-wait average for the customer service department was less than one minute during peak time. Call-wait data from each month was utilized to analyze how the customer service people could continue to maintain their standard even though call volume was on a steady 5 percent monthly increase. This is a good example of when historical data can be fed back into marketing, sales, and manufacturing organizations to determine what changes need to be made, what the issues and concerns of the customer base are, and how the issues can be resolved quickly. This particular retailer has tracked data for years. As a result, innovative products are developed and launched into the marketplace in record time.

Having baseline data ensures that performance is measured by how much incremental change has occurred. Without such data, it is really hard to tell whether your training program or any other performance improvement effort is making a difference in your organization.

If you have historical data, you can have a more valid and reliable basis for comparing your performance metrics. Having enough information also decreases the likelihood of random data spikes and errors.

Identify Long-Term Goals and Short-Term Targets

If your long-term goal is to increase sales volume by 10 percent, your short-term objectives can include activities that speed up sales, advertising methods that bring more customers in, or sales incentives that increase the percentage of closings.

The hardest part about identifying targets is determining how much improvement you want to project long range. You must make sure that a 10 percent increase in market share is realistic.

How can you know whether your targets are attainable? First, analyze historical data and identify the patterns and trends. When you use trend data to determine targets, you avoid making decisions on isolated spikes and single points of data. Study as much past information as you can. Find clear trends and patterns. The trends can be linearly increasing or decreasing, cyclical, or seasonal. For example, sales of school supplies and children's clothing gradually increase prior to the start of the school year. Retail chains project sales based on how much increase they expect every week after examining the average of the previous weeks' increases. However, once the fall semester starts, the same average weekly increase does not apply. You may also want to consider the seasonal peaks and valleys of your own data. Regardless of whether you are calculating short-term or long-term targets, the bottom line is that your targets have to be realistic and based on fact.

Tool 9 illustrates baseline data and target metrics for a typical sales organization. The framework can be used for other industries, such as manufacturing (for tracking quality data such as defect and failure rates), nonprofit organizations (for determining targets and goals for donations), and finance companies (for assessing effectiveness and efficiency of audit and accounting procedures).

Key Summary Points

The following are the key points covered in this chapter.

1. Identifying the appropriate metrics for managing your organization's performance is the cornerstone of a sound performance measurement system.
2. The three basic criteria for determining the right performance metrics include:
   - Credibility, relevance, and strategic value
   - Widely used and based on industry standards
   - Availability and accessibility
3. After identifying the right metrics, you can then collect baseline data and identify appropriate targets for each of them.

TOOL 9
DETERMINING BASELINE AND TARGET METRICS

What It's About

This tool gives you a template for collecting baseline data for your metrics as well as identifying targets for each.

Purpose of Tool

1. Provides a concrete framework for collecting baseline information and identifying appropriate target values.

2. Serves as a basis for tracking performance by comparing baseline data and targets with actual results.

How to Customize

1. Write each of the metrics you have identified in Tool 8 in the first column of this tool.

2. Then, generate current baseline data for your performance metrics from your appropriate data sources. Gather as much historical data as you can so that you can enhance the accuracy of your baseline values.

3. To identify appropriate targets, analyze your historical information for linear trends, cyclical patterns, or seasonal fluctuations. Determine where your current information lies within these trends and project your targets accordingly. For example, if current performance is in the middle of an upward cycle, then project upward targets accordingly. You also need to look at how long an average cycle takes. You can then calculate the average for the whole cycle and then estimate your target for the next cycle using this average value.

TOOL 9 (Continued)

Example

Metrics	Description of Metrics	Baseline Data	Target Goals
Sales Revenues	Total gross sales revenues per month	$600k (average during past 12 months)*	$725k (based on 20 percent growth forecast)@
Profit Margin Revenues	Total net revenues or profit margin per month	$150k (average during past 12 months)*	$180k (based on 20 percent growth forecast)@
Profit Margin Percentage	Average percent of profit margin relative to total product cost	25 percent (average during past 12 months)*	30 percent (based on current benchmarks)+
Quota Attainment	Attainment in percent per month relative to pre-set quota	108 percent (average during past 3 years)#	112 percent (based on current benchmarks)+
Close Rate	Percent of sales closed vs. total number of opportunities	20 percent (average during past 3 years)#	25 percent (based on current benchmarks)+

*Baseline averages for sales revenues, profit margin revenues, and profit margin percent are based on 12–month rolling average because of a 12–month seasonal trend. Quarterly averages fluctuate because of customer demand.

#Baseline averages for quota attainment and close rate are based on a three-year rolling average. Past historical data analysis shows average transitions in technology use, training, products, services, and tools for sales employees is approximately three years.

@Growth forecast of 20 percent is based on executive projections and economic estimates.

+Current benchmarks are determined by averaging data from exemplary and low performers.

Template

Metrics	Description of Metrics	Baseline Data	Target Goals

APPLICATION EXERCISE: CASE STUDY, CHAPTER FOUR

IDENTIFYING THE RIGHT PERFORMANCE METRICS FOR FJT TECH

Discussion: Questions and Answers

After an intensive performance analysis that was conducted by the cross-functional task force and the ROI calculation presentation as shown in the case discussion in Chapter Three, FJT Tech executives were convinced that the following four priorities needed to be implemented quickly.

- Immediately slash prices of the current product, although this will result in reduced revenues. The finance, sales, and pricing departments will work together to determine this optimum price. This has to be completed within one week.

- Invest $2M to speed up introduction of the next-generation wireless digital phone that has additional features but weighs less. The product engineering department, with support from the information technology department, will work on this, and the product will be developed three months from now.

- Introduce an advertising campaign to sustain market credibility. Estimated additional advertising cost for this effort is $1M. Marketing will work closely with sales and customer groups to identify potential audiences for this campaign. This will be implemented in conjunction with the launch of the new product in three months.

- Train sales people on new sales approach and features/benefits of the soon-to-be-released product. Estimated cost for implementing this solution is $75k. The training and performance consulting department will work closely with the different sales groups to identify commonalities and differences in the training that will be conducted for each of these business groups. Training will start two weeks prior to new product launch and advertising campaign.

With these priorities in mind and using the knowledge you have learned in this chapter, here are some questions and their answers that will help you identify the key metrics and indicators for performance measurement at FJT Tech.

1. To help FJT Tech achieve its goals of increasing market share and revenues, reducing losses, and accelerating new product development, what are the key indicators that will show that these goals have been successfully accomplished?

   By looking at these initiatives, you can then determine the key indicators that will be appropriate for FJT Tech. The suggested indicators below use the framework for Tool 6, Linking Metrics with Business Goals.

Department/ Organization	Strategic Business Goals	Projected ROI	Key Indicators/ Metrics
Sales and Finance	• Increase market share by 10% • Increase sales revenues by 30% • Increase profitability by 10% • Reduce losses by 15% at the end of the year	Benefits = $30M Cost = $2M ROI = 1,500%	• Gross sales revenues • Net revenues • Market share % • Profit margin • Sales dollars lost (actual less projected sales)
Product Engineering	• Accelerate new product development by 3 months	Benefits = $8M Cost = $2M ROI = 400%	• Process cycle time
Advertising/ Marketing	• Market new product by creating TV ads and print ads	Benefits = $2.5M Cost = $1M ROI = 250%	• Dollars spent on advertising • ROI for marketing ploys that were implemented • Forecast and actual demand

Department/ Organization	Strategic Business Goals	Projected ROI	Key Indicators/ Metrics
Training	• Up-level sales employees' knowledge and skills on selling new product	Benefits = $100k Cost = $75k ROI = 133%	• Number of sales representatives attended which training and when • Cost of training • Comparison of sales revenues and market share between those who attended the training and those who did not • ROI for new product sales training

2. Which functional areas or departments at FJT Tech are possible sources of your metrics data?

Based on the use of Tool 6 above, it looks like the data sources that have to be checked out to track key indicators will be sales and finance (for revenues, profit margin, market share percentage, and dollars invested for marketing and sales training), marketing (for types of marketing plays that were implemented during this period, forecast and actual demand, comparison of demand data for a six- to eight-week period to determine the impact of the marketing plays), and training (how many sales representatives attended which training and when, cost of training, comparison of sales revenues and market share between those who attended the training and those who did not).

3. How will you collect baseline data and target goals for the metrics you have identified earlier for FJT Tech?

To collect baseline information for each of the metrics identified in Step 1, you can use Tool 9, Determining Baseline and Target Metrics. The table below is completed to illustrate possible baseline data and target goals for each sample metric for FJT Tech, given the information in the case study so far.

Metrics	Description of Metrics	Baseline Data	Target Goals
Sales Revenues	Total gross sales revenues per month	$600k (average during past 12 months)	$725k (based on 20 percent growth forecast)
Profit Margin Revenues	Total net revenues or profit margin per month	$150k (average during past 12 months)	$180k (based on 20 percent growth forecast)
Profit Margin Percentage	Average percent of profit margin relative to total product cost	25 percent (average during past 12 months)	30 percent (based on current benchmarks)
Quota Attainment	Attainment in percent per month relative to pre-set quota	108 percent (average during past 3 years)	112 percent (based on current benchmarks)
Market Share Percentage	Percentage of potential customer market that bought FJT Tech product	21 percent (average during last 4 quarters	26 percent (based on market research study)

The assumptions on how each baseline metric was calculated follow the baseline number. The assumptions and bases for the target goals are described after the target number.

When you actually work this template for your organization, make sure you base your assumptions on realistic business expectations, data trends, industry standards, and accurate market research information. The reality is that there is some subjectivity in forecasting demand and revenue data. However, you can minimize this subjectivity by using measurement data judiciously and appropriately, for the good of the organization.

CHAPTER FIVE

IMPLEMENTING THE PERFORMANCE MEASUREMENT SYSTEM

A fter you have identified the right performance metrics to include in your measurement system, you are ready to implement it. You can generate management and stakeholder commitment to this list of metrics by consistently using them during your operations review and other business presentations. You can leverage the strategic council you created earlier to help you disseminate information about the system. You can also talk with senior executives to integrate your measures into their direct reports' performance plans. You also must influence senior management to cascade the process down to the lowest employee level. You are now in Step 3 of the performance measurement process, as shown in the model on this page.

What framework will you use to start tracking performance data? What communication methods are appropriate for delivering the results? How can you leverage technology to disseminate data quickly? How can you ensure that your data are accurate and believable? This chapter is

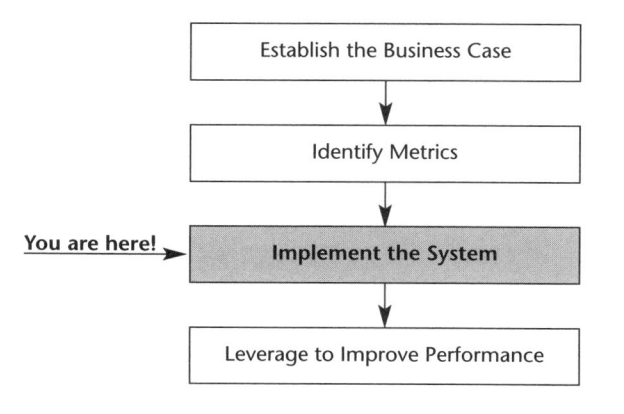

You are here! → Implement the System

- Establish the Business Case
- Identify Metrics
- Implement the System
- Leverage to Improve Performance

about implementing a performance measurement system, and we will present some tools that address these questions.

Framework for Tracking Performance Data

For your results to have relevance and value, make sure that you let your readers know the baseline values for each metric, the targets, and the current status of each. The purpose of measurement data is to provide decision makers with information on how they are doing relative to their target.

Calculating Run Rates

One of the key statistics that will help you provide current status is to calculate the *run rate* for each metric. A *run rate* shows you whether your performance in this metric is on track or not. It tells you the level you will attain relative to the goal. Your performance is on track if the run rate is 100 percent or higher, while it is not if the run rate is less than 100 percent. Before you calculate a run rate, select the appropriate time period for presenting your results: daily, weekly, monthly, quarterly, or annually. You also need to know the specific periods for which you are tracking results. For example, if sales representatives have monthly quotas and you want to determine their run rates every week, the time period is weekly and the time range for the goal is monthly. The formula for calculating a run rate is as follows:

$$\text{RUN RATE} = \text{CURRENT VALUE (PER TIME PERIOD)} \times$$
$$\text{NUMBER OF PERIODS (FOR GOAL)} / \text{TARGET GOAL}$$

Read through the following example, which shows how to calculate the run rate for sales revenues of a particular sales representative.

At the beginning of the month, baseline sales revenue is zero. This month's target quota for a sales representative is $300k, which can vary depending on the type of customer, level of experience, number and type of existing accounts, job level, and other factors. This quota translates to $15k per day, assuming that there are twenty business days per month. After one day, a sales representative generated revenues of $10k. This employee's run rate will be as shown below:

$$\text{RUN RATE} = \$10\text{K (CURRENT DAILY VALUE)} \times 20 \text{ (NUMBER OF}$$
$$\text{BUSINESS DAYS)} / \$300\text{K (TARGET)} = 0.67 \text{ OR } 67 \text{ PERCENT}$$

This means that if this sales representative's performance continues at the same rate, he or she will not achieve quota by the end of the month. For a sales organization that has seasonal patterns and varied buying cycles, such as in the example above, it may be more appropriate to track performance weekly rather than daily because of day-to-day fluctuations. In this case, if we recalculated the example on the basis of weekly data, we would find the following:

$$\text{RUN RATE} = \$90K \text{ (CURRENT WEEKLY RATE)} \times 4 \text{ (NUMBER OF WEEKS)} / \$300K \text{ (TARGET)} = 1.20 \text{ OR } 120 \text{ PERCENT}$$

If the current pace continues, the sales representative will be able achieve 120 percent of the quota for sales revenues. Having this type of information helps sales managers in coaching their respective sales teams.

Other examples are shown in Table 5.1 of how run rates can be used and how often they should be calculated. Frequency of calculation depends on factors such as size of the organization, type of product or service being provided, the nature of the target goals, and the metrics being tracked. Also consider how your organization works, how often reports are released, and how easy it is to access the data. The bottom line is that you determine what works best for your organization.

If you were calculating a run rate for a nonprofit organization in which you had targeted a certain amount of contributions for the fiscal year, you might want to calculate different segments of the customer base separately on a monthly basis. If at mid-year 90 percent of the contributions had come from one source, with the run rate showing 40 percent (10 percent short of where you should be at this point), the organization would be unlikely to meet its goal.

We once participated in a $30,000 fund-raising drive for a public radio or television program. The program targeted a combination of corporate funding, small businesses, and individuals. Once the executive director determined contributor targets, each volunteer was given a list of contributors to reach by a certain time. Run rates were given to each volunteer every three months to let them know how they were doing. Letting everybody know how well volunteers were doing relative to targets prevented the end-of-the-year rush for soliciting donations. This metric helped volunteers pace themselves better. It ensured that the campaign was successful and ran efficiently.

From our years of experience with measurement data, we have often seen the effective utilization of run rates for tracking performance. Typically, one has either a "snapshot" presentation of results in the form of a table or a pie chart or data that shows values for each week, month, quarter, or year presented in a table or graph. You can make it easy to interpret and analyze the data by showing run rates for each metric, especially if you are providing information on current status. This

TABLE 5.1. RUN RATES AND RECOMMENDED FREQUENCY OF CALCULATION

Type of Organization	Strategic Goals	Metrics	Recommended Frequency of Run Rate Calculations
Product Sales	Increase market share by 10% this year	• Market share percentage	Monthly
Manufacturing	Improve product quality by reducing defect rate to 1%	• Percentage scrap or rework	Daily
Nonprofit	Increase community participation in terms of volunteerism and donations for 1999	• Dollar donations • Number of new sponsors/ donors	Quarterly
Business/ Performance Consulting	Increase acquisition, retention, and development of customer accounts	• Number of accounts won, developed, and grown • Number of repeat business	Weekly
Software Start-up Company	Increase market capitalization	• Dollar capitalization • Stock price	Quarterly
State Auditor's Office	Increase operational efficiency	• Number of audits processed • Cycle time per audit	Monthly

Financial Investment Company	Improve customer service by reducing complaints	• Number of customer complaints • Number of repeat customer calls	Quarterly (can be monthly)
Television Company	Increase viewership	• Average Nielsen rating	Weekly

metric provides a way to know quickly whether the unit is performing well or not. With the limited time that executives have for viewing reports, using run rates is a good way to show level of performance at a given time.

Tool 10 presents a framework for presenting baseline data and tracking performance relative to pre-set targets.

To help you analyze current performance, change is indicated by a (+) for an increase or performance improvement or a (–) for a decrease in performance. The run rate shows your end result if you maintain the current level of performance. In the customer service example shown in Tool 10, you can see that the customer service representative is doing well in terms of the quality metrics of the job. However, the person is not doing well on the close rate. The number of calls handled and number of problems solved during first calls are below target, but as a manager I might just remind the representative to handle a few more calls per day. This is a good example of a balanced scorecard, where both quantity and quality measures are included.

Methods for Communicating Results

You can deliver your performance measurement report using a variety of methods. To choose the method appropriate for your organization, consider size of your audience, job nature (physical or knowledge workers), work configuration (field or office), and your technology infrastructure. For example, if you want to send measurement reports to 1,500 managers in your organization, it may be practical to use the web, as long as all the managers have access to it. Using the web is also practical for sending reports to knowledge workers who use computers on the job and to field-based personnel who have dial-up networking capabilities. If you generate reports that need to be communicated to your top executives, then it is

TOOL 10

FRAMEWORK FOR TRACKING PERFORMANCE DATA

What It's About

This tool provides a framework for identifying baseline values of each of your performance metrics, determining appropriate targets, and tracking current performance relative to those targets.

Purpose of Tool

1. Presents a consistent framework for assessing current performance status.

2. Provides an objective basis for determining coaching and other performance improvement opportunities.

How to Customize

1. Make sure you use the right metrics and targets, using the process described earlier in Chapter Four.

2. You can use this framework as a tracking system for your sales, financial, manufacturing, and other functional metrics. Revise the different rows and columns appropriately to reflect your organization's needs.

3. Make sure you always include the run rate for each metric. Before you calculate this run rate, decide on the appropriate time period that you want to track for each metric (i.e., daily, weekly, monthly, quarterly). Be practical and consider what makes the most sense to the people who will be receiving this data.

Example

Name of Sales Rep: _____ For Week 2: _____

Manager Name: _____

Metrics	Current Averages	Target Goal for Month	Current Value for Week	Run Rate
Sales Revenues	$600k	$725k	$400k	$800k (+)
Profit Margin Revenues	$150k	$180k	$100k	$200k (+)
Profit Margin Percentage	25%	30%	29%	33% (+)
Close Rate	20%	25%	22%	24% (−)

Customer Service Example

Name of Sales Rep: _____ For Day 2: _____

Manager Name: _____

Metrics	Current Daily Averages	Target Goal for Week	Current Value for Day	Run Rate
Calls Handled	56	230	54	220 (−)
Calls Solved During First Call	25	125	23	115 (−)
Repeat Calls (Same Customer)	9	45	6	30 (+)
Calls Diagnosed Accurately	49	245	50	250 (+)

$$\text{Run Rate} = \frac{\text{Current Value (per time period)} \times \text{Number of Periods (for goal)}}{\text{Target Goal}}$$

Template

Name of Sales Rep: _____   For Week 2: _____

Manager Name: _____

Metrics	Current Averages	Target Goal for Month	Current Value for Week	Run Rate

Run Rate = Current Value/Number of Weeks Elapsed × Number of Weeks

better to either send a hard copy of an executive summary, conduct PowerPoint®️ presentations, or talk one-on-one with each of them. Finally, if you want to share the results of an evaluation study you conducted on the effectiveness of a sales training course, you may want to consider publishing the results in your organization's newsletter.

Tool 11 provides a resource for selecting the right media for your performance measurement system. It gives examples for each medium of delivery, as well as appropriate situations when each medium can be best utilized.

What to Communicate

Now that you have decided on *how* to communicate your results, let us look at what you need to include in your report. The content for your report depends on your audience and the value of the information, the time that your audience has available to read it, and the degree of presentation detail. If your readers are the company's executives, then generate an executive summary that provides a big picture view of the data so they can see the performance trends and impact right away. With executives and decision makers, be ready with a three-minute snapshot view of results or a simple visual graphic that shows performance status. You may also want to consider preparing a thirty-second spiel that you can use when the opportunity arises.

If your report is on a research study that you conducted to measure the impact of a training course on your business, then make sure you have a one-page executive summary and a detailed report. Include the purpose and method used in the study, key findings, and recommendations, with emphasis on suggestions that your audience has the authority to make decisions about. There is no sense in including recommendations that your readers cannot use.

The detailed report on the research project mentioned above should contain the following:

Overview. This section should explain the purpose and business reasons for the research project. Also describe the objectives of the training program or performance activity that you are trying to measure.

Methodology. This section should describe the population and sample size, sampling procedure, data design used (pre-and post-training group and control group or pre- and post-training group only), demographic comparisons (if training and control groups are used), data collection method (survey, e-mail, business data analysis), and response rate (if applicable).

TOOL 11

SELECTING THE RIGHT MEDIA FOR COMMUNICATING RESULTS

What It's About

This tool provides a framework for determining the right medium for delivering measurement results. It will help you make a decision on the appropriate method to use by using specific criteria.

Purpose of Tool

1. Presents a criteria for determining the appropriate media to use for reporting.

2. Suggests a list of different methods for communicating results to different audiences.

How to Customize

1. Before you use the tool, make sure you identify the different audiences for each of the measurement reports that you are building.

2. Conduct some research on all the different modes of communication that are available in your organization. If they exist, leverage on them so you don't have to reinvent the wheel.

3. Let your strategic measurement council, if you have one in place, make the decision on appropriate methods of communicating your data.

Example

Medium	Delivery Methods	When to Use It
Technology	• Web-based reports • E-mail • Online newsletter or magazine • CD-ROM	• Audience has access to technology • Audience knows how to use technology • Enterprise-wide delivery coverage • Report covers general company-wide information • Reports are for broad-based, general audiences • Appropriate for field-based employees who have networking capabilities • Communicate results globally from a central-ized location
Hard Copy Reports	• Binder/manual reports • Newsletter • Bulletin board announcements • Company magazine or journal	• Not all target audiences have access to or knows how to use technology • Appropriate for audiences with mobile jobs who have no networking capabilities • Targeted only for a specific department or business unit • Reports are for specific, small audiences
Oral Presentation	• Operations review meetings • Department/team meetings • One-on-one meeting	• Need to have audience make decisions related to data • Targeted only for a specific team or individual • Reports are for specific, small audiences

Template

Medium	Delivery Methods	When to Use It
Technology		
Hard Copy Reports		
Oral Presentation		

Data Results. Summarize the data in tables, charts, or graphs in this section. For open-ended information, try to group common comments by counting frequencies for each group. Comments that have frequencies of 10 percent or more are worth mentioning in the analysis and should have at least one recommendation for addressing any opportunities for improvement. Include some interpretation and analysis of the results here as well.

Conclusions and Recommendations. Generate conclusions and recommendations by focusing on data trends and key comments. Identify recommendations that can be acted on by your reader or audience. You can also cite the implications of this project on other areas of the business. For example, if you conducted a sales impact study of a sales negotiation course, develop some suggestions on how the results can help marketing, finance, customer service, and other business units in your organization. This is a good opportunity for you to show how your efforts integrate with other areas of the business.

Using Technology to Communicate Results

We have used examples and situations in which using technology, hard copies, or presentations is appropriate. Using technology is also a feasible way to report results in a fast-paced environment. When measurement reporting is linked with what the business does, providing data instantaneously is a huge competitive advantage for the organization. For example, for just-in-time manufacturing organizations, providing current, real-time information on sales order and inventory status is critical. Because there are no huge inventories for parts and components, it is imperative that manufacturing employees who are directly involved with processing customer orders have access to parts availability. In this way, serious customer dissatisfaction issues can be prevented.

Optimizing the use of technology for delivering measurement results has many advantages. Among them are:

Data Accuracy and Integrity. If your company has well-established databases for finance, sales, and employee information, you can generate reports using a technology-driven tool from this database. Getting the data straight from the source ensures its accuracy and integrity.

Consistency and Standardization. Using a well-designed, consistent, standard framework for reporting measurement data means you will be able to make comparisons and analyze trends better. You can track performance over time so that you can know how well you are doing relative to yesterday, last week, or last year. Using a consistent method also implies that you will be able to forecast needs and performance better because you have objective data on which to base your projections.

Ease of Maintenance. The hardest part about using technology for reporting is designing it the first time. Once you have laid the framework, it is relatively easy to maintain. If data in the source database changes, the reports automatically change. You do need to make sure that you work closely with the people who maintain the source database (for example, sales operations, finance departments, HR database operations) so you can report data discrepancies.

Flexibility. Using technology for reporting provides you with some flexibility. Most reporting tools and database applications allow you to change the visual presentation of your data quickly. In fact, you can generate different tables, graphs, and so forth, depending on what your audience prefers.

Accessibility. For those who have access to and know how to use technology, web reports are easily downloadable. Web reporting has gone a long way in making reports more user friendly.

Global Availability. If you have a global organization, using technology for reporting can help bridge the geographic distance. Of course, the other global regions you are trying to reach must have the bandwidth and technology resources to access the results quickly and efficiently. Your regional clients must also meet the minimum standards required to access and run applications that you are using. For example, minimum requirements for operating system version, modem speed, Internet browser version, and software application standards have to be considered.

Integration with Other Data Systems. Using technology for reporting also gives you an opportunity to integrate measurement into your other existing information systems in the organization. Employee information systems, sales tracking systems, and financial data systems are examples of organizational information systems that you can use in building your reports. Identify the nature, hardware and software architecture, programming language, and maintenance requirements of these existing systems at the outset to ensure that your technology-based reports are compatible with them.

Once you have decided that using technology is appropriate for you and your organization, there are some other major factors that you need to consider. Among these are the following:

Database-Driven Technology. When looking for the right software tool for your measurement system, make sure that the data and content in the tool are stored systematically in a database. Check with your information technology department to find out what database systems are supported in the organization. Otherwise, you might end up with a database that cannot be maintained and supported.

Technical Certification Processes. An example of one of these processes is Y2K certification, which entails running data reports to ensure that your tool can recognize the year 2000 as distinct from 1900. This enhances the integrity of the data in your measurement system.

System Development Life Cycle. Work in conjunction with your information technology organization, presenting your business case, analyzing the needs of your audience, determining the escalation process for technical support, describing the hardware requirements, conceptualizing the data structure, and working out other systems-related issues. Also, leverage your IT team's technical expertise by following standard requirements and processes.

Compatibility with Existing Systems. Ensure that your reporting tool is compatible with other existing systems. When deciding on a tool, check what other systems you need to interface with so that you can report on all the data sources that are available. If you belong to the training or learning department, make sure the tool can interface with your registration, scheduling, evaluation, and student tracking system so you can generate reports on how many attended what course, number and cost of no-shows, and roll-up summaries for departments, segments, and other work groups.

Maintenance Issues. Make sure to address maintenance issues up-front. When building the tool initially, ensure that you have a maintenance plan in place. Build in the cost of maintenance so you don't have to scurry for resources later. Examples of what has to be included in the maintenance plan include upgrades in technology, server hardware bandwidth, security access and permissions, and database migration changes.

Training for Users. Design and develop training for report administrators and users alike. Before you even select and implement the tool, develop a plan for training employees who will be involved in designing and generating reports. Also, make sure you have a process for training your data users and other audiences for the reports. The type, content breadth, and duration of the training may vary from one group to another. You may also want to build in an online training tool for users who can learn at their own pace. Other groups may need a job aid that describes the basic functionalities of the tool and a simple "how to" guide.

Scalability and Flexibility. Make sure your reports are scalable and flexible enough for a diverse range of users. The type of reports appropriate for a given audience can vary depending on technical skills, access to technology, and use of data on the job. Build a cafeteria menu with all possible choices of formats (table, pie chart, line graph, bar chart, scatter diagram) and data fields (employee name, manager name, sales revenue, courses attended, job family) so your users can pick and choose those that are appropriate for them. Provide options by building in flexibility in your report outputs and data formats.

Cost Considerations. Conduct a cost-benefit analysis for a site license, enterprise license, or individual licenses. Analyze short-and long-term benefits of the tool. Implementing technologies always requires initial investments up-front, so make sure you project benefits of using the technology toward the life cycle of the tool.

Tool 12 provides a checklist of factors you must consider when using technology for measurement reporting. Find out about the pieces you already have and what else is missing so you know what your next steps should be.

Ensuring Data Accuracy and Integrity

Your measurement system will only be as good as your data. Your clients are sensitive to data accuracy issues, so make sure that you have mechanisms in place that support the integrity of your information. The key to ensuring data accuracy and integrity is to use source data for reporting. As much as possible, report data from the original source, because second-hand information may not be accurate. Take some time to identify the key data sources in your organization and the people who control them. Establish a good relationship with database administrators and programmers who can provide you with much-needed troubleshooting support later on.

◆ ◆ ◆

Key Summary Points

The following are the key points covered in this chapter.

1. Develop a consistent, easy-to-interpret framework for tracking performance data. Provide meaningful information that is easily understood so that decisions can be made based on data.
2. When selecting the right method for communicating results, consider audience factors such as technology and Internet access, size, nature of work, and type of decisions that will be made.
3. Among the requirements for using technology for implementing your performance measurement system are data accuracy, ease of maintenance, consistency, accessibility, flexibility, global availability, and integration with other information systems.

TOOL 12

TECHNOLOGY CHECKLIST FOR MEASUREMENT REPORTING

What It's About

This tool provides a list of suggested requirements for successfully using technology for your measurement system. Use this tool to assess opportunities for improvement in your organization.

Purposes of Tool

1. Presents a list of requirements for using technology in performance measurement.

2. Provides some initial next steps for addressing each opportunity for improvement.

How to Customize

1. If you can't answer all the items in this checklist (which is understandable), think of people and departments in the different business units who can provide these answers. Since this is a technology checklist, the first place to start will be your IT or IS department.

2. This is your opportunity to establish (or enhance) your relationships with your IT/IS partners. It is imperative that you value their expertise by soliciting their support and involvement throughout your project.

3. Follow the recommended initial steps in the areas you need to improve.

Example

Requirements	Example for Selected Tool
Capabilities	• Standard and ad hoc reporting • Roll-up/ roll-down of reports, cross-tabs, charts (currently for advanced client license only, but upgraded version to be released later this year will include this) • Static/dynamic
Database technology	• Oracle, Sybase • Microsoft SQL
Compatibility with existing systems	• Survey tool • HR employee database • Business data warehouse • Testing tool • Project tracking tool
Maintenance/ sustaining issues	Easily maintained since database-driven, IT maintains central database
Training required	Minimal; user licensees to be determined
Scalability	Very scalable, enterprise-wide tool
Flexibility/ customization	Contingent on level and type of customization, need to ask whether it has capability to integrate prescriptive recommendations and tools to metric analysis
Extent of your team's involvement	Initial database setup, work with technical consultants, design interface, identify security access levels
IT support	Fully supported, system development cycle process underway
Cost: site license, procurement, single user/ multiple user	• Full client (more functionality and advanced reporting capabilities) or web client • Dollar installation fee + consultant setup time + dollar per user (administrative) + dollar per user for Excel plug-in
IT contacts	• Project manager • HR IT manager • HR production database consultant
Vendor project manager/contact	• Put name here

TOOL 12 (Continued)

Template

Requirements	Example for Selected Tool
Capabilities	
Database technology	
Compatibility with existing systems	
Maintenance/ sustaining issues	
Training required	
Scalability	
Flexibility/ customization	
Extent of Internal Involvement	
IT support	
Cost: site license, procurement, single user/ multiple user	
IT contacts	

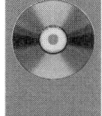

APPLICATION EXERCISE: CASE STUDY, CHAPTER FIVE

IMPLEMENTING THE PERFORMANCE MEASUREMENT SYSTEM AT FJT TECH

Discussion: Questions and Answers

Now you know the departments that are responsible for achieving certain business goals and the key metrics that will be used to measure their performance. The one metric that management is particularly interested in monitoring is the sales department's sales revenues. You know that you can be helpful in setting up a tracking mechanism for this and other related sales data. Using the knowledge you have learned in this chapter, here are some questions and their answers that will help you implement a global performance measurement system at FJT Tech.

1. What framework will you use to track and manage performance sales data at FJT Tech, now that you have identified the right metrics?

   The structure provided in Tool 10, Framework for Tracking Performance Data, will be a good start for FJT Tech. The key elements in this framework have to be there: metric, current average, target goal for month (or a specified period), current performance level, and run rate. What you know about FJT Tech is the following:

Metric	Current Average	Target Goal for Month
Sales Revenue	$600k	$725k
Profit Margin Revenues	$150k	$180k

   Each of these elements is essential in analyzing whether FJT Tech is in the right direction relative to these metrics. Below is a sample framework that can work for FJT Tech. To complete this, you would enter the current value for this week and calculate the run rate using the formula given. Positive run rates indicate that performance is in the right direction, while a negative run rate signifies a need for coaching and feedback to improve performance.

Exercise

Please complete the information below. If current values for this week for each metric are given in the table, calculate the run rate for each of these metrics. Run rate answers are shown at the back of this section.

Name of Sales Rep: _____   For Week 2: _____

Manager Name: _____

Metrics	Current Averages	Target Goal for Month	Current Value for Week 1	Run Rate
Sales Revenues	$600k	$725k	$180k	
Profit Margin Revenues	$150k	$180k	$45k	

$$\text{Run Rate} = \frac{\text{Current Value (per time period)} \times \text{Number of Periods (for goal)}}{\text{Target Goal}}$$

2. How will measurement data be communicated to FJT Tech employees? Who can benefit from this information? When should it be delivered to these audiences?

   After having a consistent framework for delivering measurement results, you can use Tool 11, Selecting the Right Media for Communicating Results, to come up with your media selection plan. Here is a strategy that can work for FJT Tech.

Medium	Examples	When to Use It
Technology	• Web-based reports	• FJT Tech is a high-tech company, so these methods will work for sales, marketing, and finance managers and directors for viewing their team's performance • These reports can be refreshed weekly or monthly • Because FJT Tech is a global

		company, using web-based reports will be appropriate
Hard Copy Reports	• Weekly paper reports	• As a back-up to the web reports, these hard-copy reports can be provided at the desks of sales managers at the start of the week • Roll-up reports for teams, departments, segments, and business units can be provided to the various managers who have responsibilities for each of these audience groups
Oral Presentation	• Department/ team meetings	• One-on-one meeting • For directors, VPs, and the cross-functional task force, one-on-one meetings, or team presentations will be appropriate for sharing these results. • Hard-copy reports will also be appropriate here. Most executives are rarely in their offices to view the web reports.

3. If FJT Tech decides to use technology for reporting measurement results, what factors do you have to consider? How can you ensure that the use of the technology is effective and efficient?

   You can answer these questions by using Tool 12, Technology Checklist for Measurement Reporting. By completing this checklist, you increase your chances of deploying this tool successfully at FJT Tech.

Requirements	Criteria for Selecting Reporting Tool
Capabilities	• Standard and ad hoc reporting capability is important so sales managers can query specific fields and data • Roll-up summary reports have to be available so comparisons can be done • Web reports and Excel downloadable spreadsheets are needed so audience can customize their own reports
Database technology	• Make sure you check the database system that your sales data sources at FJT Tech use so the selected tool is compatible with this database format (i.e., Access, Oracle, SQL)
Compatibility with existing systems	• If your measurement data requires different data sources, make sure your tool is able to integrate these data sources. If possible, use a well-structured data warehouse to run reports • Examples of data sources you have at FJT Tech are the HR employee database, sales and financial data, and training activity data
Maintenance/ sustaining issues	• Make sure the tool is self-sustaining and easy to maintain • Leverage existing IT resources who can support the tool
Training required	• Identify all your audiences—users, managers, performance consultants, trainers, etc., who need to be trained on the application of the tool • Check with the vendor for the training and documentation that they provide as part of the purchase
Scalability	• Make sure that the tool is scalable as your organization grows and expands

Flexibility/customization	• Contingent upon level and type of customization, determine whether the tool has capability to integrate prescriptive recommendations and statistical analysis
IT support	• Partner with your IT/IS/MIS department to assess how much support they can provide
Cost: site license, procurement, single user/multiple user	• Check on licensing and costs for installation, consultant setup time, administrative, and other related expenses • Conduct a cost-benefit analysis for the different options
IT contacts	• Make sure you include IT contacts as part of the technology team. This should include the IT project manager and the production database consultant

Answer to Question 1: Run Rate Calculations

Name of Sales Rep: _____   For Week 2: _____

Manager Name: _____

Metrics	Current Averages	Target Goal for Month	Current Value for Week 1	Run Rate
Sales Revenues	$600k	$725k	$180k	$720k (99%)
Profit Margin Revenues	$150k	$180k	$45k	$180k (100%)

Run Rate = Current Value (per time period) × Number of Periods (for goal)

$$\frac{\text{Target Goal}}{}$$

Sales Revenues	= $180k x 4 weeks / $725k
	= $720k / $725k = 99 percent
Profit Margin Revenues	= $45k x 4 weeks / $180k
	= $180k / $180k = 100 percent

This particular sales representative is right on target, although there is a lot of room for improvement in terms of exceeding goals.

CHAPTER SIX

LEVERAGING RESULTS TO IMPROVE PERFORMANCE

In the previous chapter, we discussed the various methods of communication available to you for sharing results within your organization. In some of the communications you may present only raw data, and in others you may present an analysis and interpretation of the data, followed by recommendations for action. Or you may follow up at a meeting with key management to discuss your results and want to give a summary, analysis, and recommendations. You are now in the last step of the performance measurement process, as seen in the model on this page.

In this chapter we will review in depth the various strategies available to you for analyzing and interpreting your data. In addition, we will share our thoughts on how you can leverage your measurement data to improve performance within the company.

Interpretation of results and leveraging of data are critical for continuous performance improvement. They are ways to provide

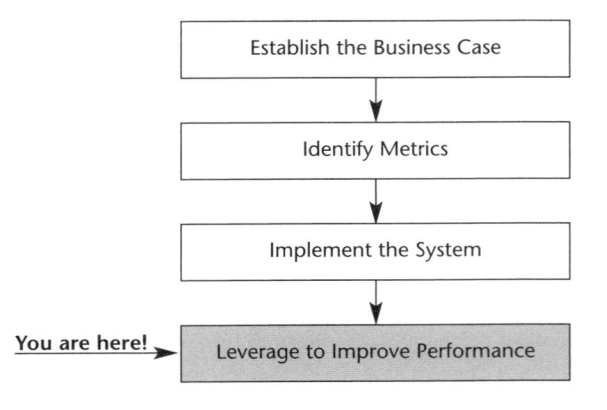

objective justification for making decisions related to improving performance. They can also provide concrete data to identify causes of performance problems.

For example, a sales representative's monthly run rate can help a sales manager determine the coaching that is appropriate for the person. If the run rate exceeds the goal for the particular period, then the manager can talk to the person regarding the things the representative did well. Performance has to be benchmarked and documented so that other sales representatives can replicate whatever led to this exemplary performance. The manager should also reinforce the person's performance so it can be sustained or improved. On the other hand, if the run rate is under 100 percent, it indicates the need for the manager to coach the employee and for them to jointly identify strategies for improving performance.

A key reason for leveraging measurement results is to use them to identify opportunities for performance improvement. A performance measurement system that presents current status on key indicators can help line managers and other decision makers identify gaps in performance. Current data and historical data can be used to project desired goals.

Sharing measurement results and interpreting them is not enough. The data must be easy to understand and intuitive. Analyze the data using the language of your business so that managers and others can relate to what you are saying. Only then can you truly say that you are helping your audience make objective, data-based decisions.

Strategies for Presenting Data

Results must be presented in a succinct and impactful way. Capsulize voluminous information into one or two key messages that reflect the meaning of the data for your audience and give others a clear way to make decisions. In the sales example above, if your audience is the manager of the sales representative, then you may want to present the results in a table that shows actual revenue, profit margin, or quotas attained and the run rate for each of these. It is important for the sales manager to see a balanced set of measures for each representative and across all representatives in the department. If someone's performance in other measures is also below the expected run rate, then it is significant enough to warrant talking with the representative about possible causes. The manager and representative can mutually discuss how to address these issues, and the manager can coach the representative appropriately.

On the other hand, if the run rate for revenues is lower than 100 percent but those of margin and quota attainment exceed 100 percent, then there may be no cause for alarm. Random fluctuations are a part of the sales business. That is why a balanced set of measures must be identified up-front.

Another possible audience for the weekly sales performance report described above could be the marketing group. How you present run rate results to this group should be different from how you present it to the sales manager. Marketing's interest can be to assess whether the marketing efforts that were played out during the prior week are working. Another measure that can be included in the representative's scorecard in a sales organization is "marketing code captures," which tell the number and percentage of orders attributed to a particular marketing effort. This can help the marketing group identify the most effective strategies as they plan for the future. Always let your sales representatives know that you expect them to capture this data, and be sure to reward them for doing so. This is a perfect example of how different functional units can work together for the good of the organization.

What are some strategies for presenting data and when do you use them? Strategies can be categorized in terms of the number of dimensions that they present. One-dimensional methods present data as a "snapshot." If presented for just one time period, revenue, volume, turnover rate, or customer satisfaction is considered one-dimensional. Two-dimensional strategies are those that present a metric over a period of time. Time is considered the second dimension. An example of a two-dimensional presentation method is a bar chart that shows turnover rate every month for four months. Such a chart gives you a good perspective on whether turnover rate is increasing, decreasing, or just fluctuating randomly. The more periods of time you present, the more conclusive your analysis will be in terms of data trends.

One-Dimensional Techniques

Data Tables. Data tables are appropriate for a "snapshot in time" presentation of data. Here, you present results only for a specified period of time—daily, weekly, monthly, quarterly, or annually—without comparing results from previous periods. This type of comparative analysis is best presented in visual format such as line graphs and bar charts, rather than in data tables, so that the information can be processed easily.

In Figure 6.1, for example, comparative assessment test scores are presented as a data table and percentage of correct responses per item as a line graph. The table shows the differences in test results of various groups in a product marketing class. The percentage of participation, average score, and average scores for specific job titles are shown for each group of students. A table is appropriate for presenting this data because the metrics reflect one-time results, immediately after the test was given. You can compare test scores among job families horizontally while comparing scores among student groups vertically. You can easily see significant differences among test scores across job families and student groups.

On the other hand, the line graph in Figure 6.1 shows the percentage of students taking a product sales test who answered each test question correctly. The graph shows that the questions have varying levels of difficulty.

FIGURE 6.1. SAMPLE DATA TABLE AND LINE GRAPH

	Percent Participation	Average Score	Field Reps	Acct Mgrs	Sales Reps	Sales Mgrs	Sup Reps
All Groups	64.1%	12.8					
Large Accounts	68.8%	13.2	13.7	13.5	12.6	14.2	
Medium Accounts	60.5%	12.7	12.7	14.1	12.5	12.2	
Small Accounts	80.8%	12.3	13.2	12	11.7	14.3	
System Support	20.7%	13.3					14.6

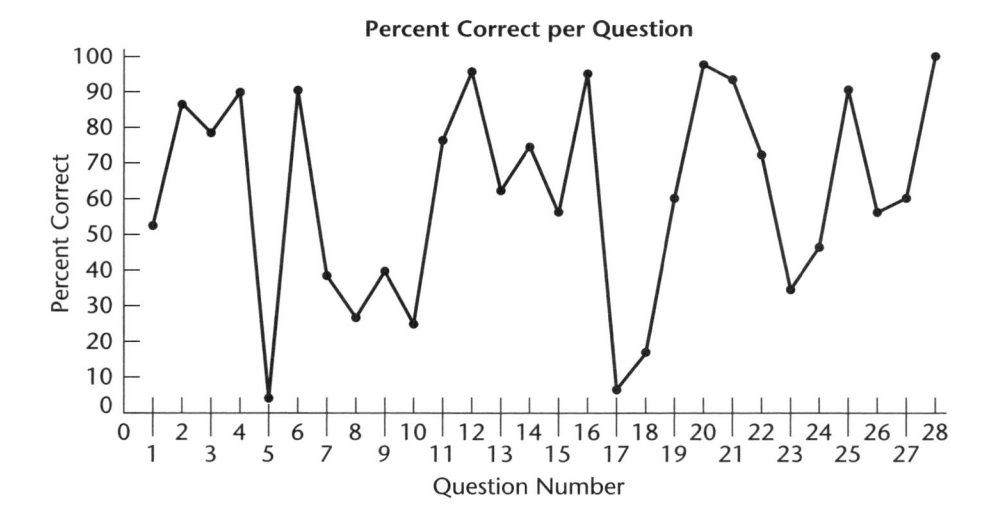

Pie Charts. Pie charts are similar to data tables in terms of their being a "snapshot in time." This format is useful for showing data distribution and breakdown. You could easily show the percentage of each type of marketing code captured in the earlier example by using a pie chart. Pie charts provide a quick, easy-to-interpret view of data.

For example, for a nonprofit organization you could use a pie chart to show a demographic distribution of how much each region in the country contributed to an annual fund-raising effort. The reader could quickly see the level of contribution of each region relative to the overall nationwide total.

One disadvantage of using pie charts is that they cannot be used to show comparative data over time, as the pie represents 100 percent of the results at one point in time. Therefore, pie charts cannot be used to describe trends or to forecast future performance. Although they are visually appealing and easy to understand, they do not provide the depth of analysis that you need for performance improvement.

An example of a good use for pie charts is shown in Figure 6.2. This pie chart shows the distribution of categories of training in terms of total student hours. Compared to the same data presented in a table, the pie chart has more impact and is easier to interpret. The pie chart clearly shows that training of new hires comprises almost half the training hours. Finding this information in the table is not as simple. Using different colors for sections of the pie adds visual appeal.

Two-Dimensional Strategies

Graphs. Graphs are visual displays that can be used to organize and summarize data. They are typically the simplest and best way of analyzing, understanding, and communicating data. For performance measurement, they can be used to illustrate current performance, identify a problem area, or present new, improved performance. Among the most commonly used type of graph is the line graph. Tool 13 can help you to construct a line graph.

On your graph, the y axis can represent the metric (revenue, profit, volume, dollars generated, customer satisfaction) and the vertical axis can be time. The points on the chart then illustrate the value of the metric for a certain period of time, whether daily, weekly, monthly, or annually.

A line graph is shown in Figure 6.3. The graph shows units sold for the first eleven weeks of 1997 by type of account, big, medium, or small. Looking at the three lines shows that the number of units sold for each of the customer segments is increasing. This analysis would not have been easily made if the data were presented as they are in Figure 6.4, as a simple table.

FIGURE 6.2. SAMPLE PIE CHART

		No. of Students	Student Hours	Tuition	Hours/ Student	$$/Hr
FY98	New Hire	2,789	132,103	$206,701	47.4	$1.56
FY98	Job Basics	13,300	42,092	$379,454	3.2	$9.01
FY98	Sales	7,648	30,117	$1,518,382	3.9	$50.42
FY98	Management Skills	3,580	17,739	$434,712	5.0	$24.51
FY98	Business Needs	3,684	35,690	$834,344	9.7	$23.38
FY98	Other + External	3,089	27,321	$705,783	8.8	$25.83

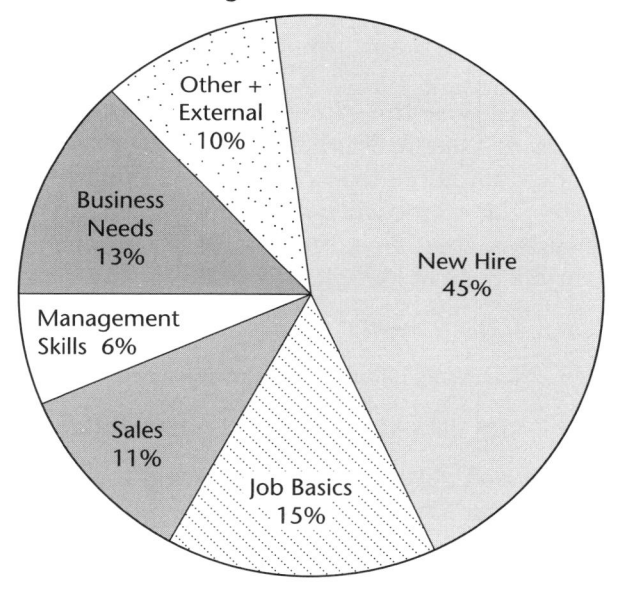

What Training Do We Deliver? FY98 YTD

TOOL 13

CONSTRUCTING A LINE GRAPH

What It's About

A line graph is a visual display of the pattern of data.

Purpose of Tool

A line graph is primarily used for:

1. Comparing two or more variables,

2. Identifying problem areas by looking at the high and low points of the graph, and

3. Outlining patterns and behavior of data.

How to Customize

To build a line graph, you can follow these basic steps:

Step 1: Choose the variable/metric to be measured. These metrics should be those indicators that you identified as key to the success of your organization. Only one metric should be represented in one line graph. This metric will be plotted on the y axis. Choose the controlled variable, such as time, that the variable will be measured against. This controlled variable is plotted along the x axis.

Step 2: Collect the data.

Step 3: Label and scale the x and y axes.

Step 4: Plot the data and connect the data points with a straight line.

Special Note: Steps 3 and 4 can be done easily using a number of spreadsheet applications and computer packages such as Excel, SAS, and SPSS. To learn where to obtain these software applications, see the resource listing at the end of this book.

Template for a Line Graph

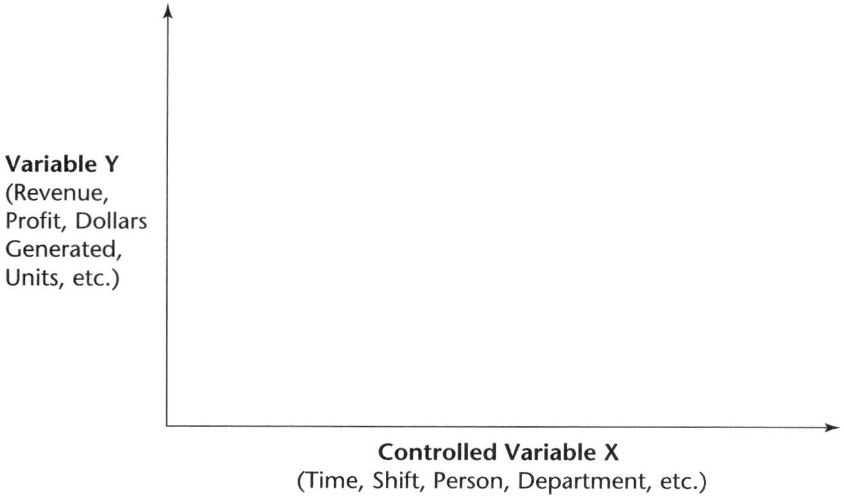

Variable Y
(Revenue,
Profit, Dollars
Generated,
Units, etc.)

Controlled Variable X
(Time, Shift, Person, Department, etc.)

FIGURE 6.3. LINE GRAPH SHOWING UNITS SOLD BY ACCOUNT

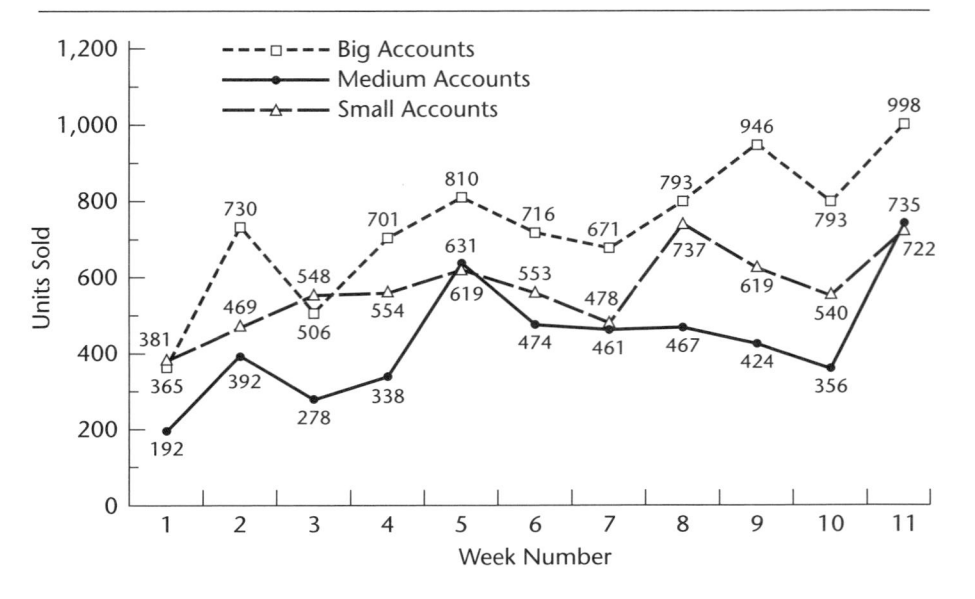

It is clear from these two figures that comparison data on a data table is not as powerful and easy-to-interpret a tool as a line graph. Differences across groups and trends are much easier to see on a line graph. Use them in your executive summaries. Remember that data tables are not appropriate for presenting comparisons and trends.

Trend Line Analysis. Trend line analysis is an extension of a line graph. This method involves identifying a line that best "fits" the points on the chart. A trend line actually represents the rate at which your chosen metric changes per unit of time. For example, if revenue points are $30k, $43k, and $51k for three consecutive weeks, the trend line is measured by determining the difference between $51k (last week) and $30k (first week), which is $21k, divided by the number of weeks, which is 3. See the formula below.

$$\text{TREND LINE} = \$51\text{K} - \$30\text{K} / 3 = \$7\text{K PER WEEK}$$

Hence, the rate at which revenue increases per week is $7k. Trend measures are valuable if you want to forecast revenues for the next quarter or for the whole year. You can use this rate to project future performance. In the example shown in Figure 6.4, you can calculate the trend line by using the process described above. Subtract the last period observation from the first period data and divide by the

FIGURE 6.4. DATA TABLE SHOWING UNITS SOLD BY ACCOUNT

	Customer Group		
Week #	Big Accounts[*]	Small Accounts[@]	Medium Accounts[#]
1	381	385	192
2	730	469	392
3	548	506	278
4	701	554	338
5	810	631	619
6	716	553	474
7	671	478	461
8	793	737	467
9	946	619	424
10	793	540	356
11	998	735	722

[*]Big Accounts = Customer companies with more than 5,000 employees
[#]Medium Accounts = Customer companies with 2,000 to 4,999 employees
[@]Small Accounts = Customer companies with less than 2,000 employees

number of periods. Then plot the trend line between the two lines to see where you are going.

This method is only applicable if your data has only one general trend. If you have a lot of data points, you may have more than one trend line. In this case, you may have to calculate multiple trend lines and make your projections accordingly. A concrete example of having more than one trend would be sales revenues where trends vary by quarter because of seasonal fluctuations. In sales organizations, projections for the first quarter of the next year are determined by looking at the trend line for the first quarter of the previous year. Such seasonal trends always have to be taken into account to make your data analysis valid.

An example is shown in Figure 6.5 of an increasing trend line for the number of units sold for low-end products. To determine the weekly rate at which units are sold, you can do this calculation:

$$\text{TREND LINE} = 669 \text{ UNITS} - 207 \text{ UNITS} / 11 \text{ WEEKS} = 462 / 11 = 42 \text{ UNITS/WEEK}$$

If this trend continues, the forecast for Week 12 should be approximately

FIGURE 6.5. NUMBER OF UNITS SOLD
BY WEEK AND PRODUCT LEVEL

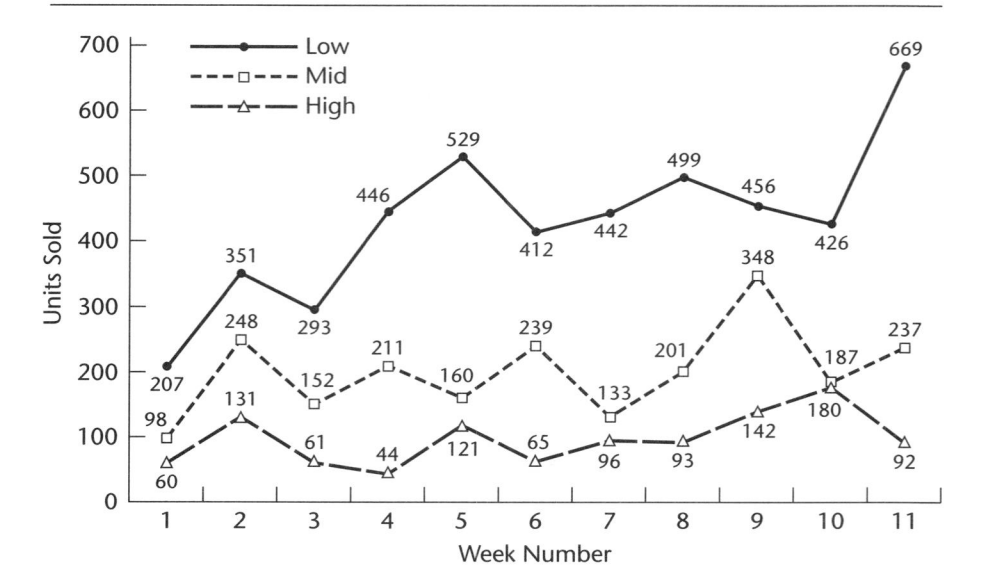

WEEK 11 UNITS + TREND LINE = 669 + 42 = 711 UNITS

The same method can be used for forecasting future weeks.

The use of trend line analysis has been simplified here to illustrate its value in forecasting future performance. In reality, business data may not have a perfectly linear trend. There can be cyclical patterns or seasonal trends over a defined period of time. In such cases, you can utilize more complex forecasting techniques. You can learn more about these complex techniques in production operations and business management books. See the resource listing at the end of this book.

Cause-Effect Diagrams. Another powerful tool for performance measurement is the cause-effect diagram, also known as the Ishikawa or fishbone diagram.

A cause-effect diagram for the example we have been using of a sales organization is shown in Figure 6.6. For purposes of this figure, the desired effect is *higher close rate.* We worked with a focus group composed of a sales manager and five sales representatives to identify the major "bones" in this diagram. The focus group identified technique, process, product being sold, environment, and management as the major categories. The factors under each category that were selected by the focus group included the following:

TOOL 14

CONSTRUCTING A CAUSE-EFFECT DIAGRAM

What It's About

A cause-effect (CE) diagram is used to show the relationship between a given effect and all identified causes of the effect. It is a qualitative method of presenting data that does not involve numerical measures. In performance measurement, this can be used to identify the possible reasons behind poor performance. Conversely, it can be utilized to determine the factors behind exemplary performance that need to be benchmarked.

Purpose of Tool

A CE diagram can assist a line manager or performance consultant in:

1. Gathering and organizing the possible causes of a situation or a desired state;

2. Reaching a common understanding of the situation through group brainstorming and consensus;

3. Exposing gaps in existing knowledge about factors that impact a desired consequence;

4. Ranking the most probable causes through group analysis; and

5. Studying the subcauses of each major cause.

How to Customize

To ensure that your CE diagram is accurate, many different perspectives are needed. The best means to achieve this is brainstorming with representatives from all functional areas involved or affected by the situation or the performance problem. The steps involved in building this diagram are:

Step 1: Clearly define the performance problem (or desired consequence) to be studied. Keep the problem or consequence as brief as possible to avoid confusion and keep everyone focused.

TOOL 14 (Continued)

Step 2: Draw a broad arrow going from left to right. This is the "backbone" of the diagram. Write the effect or problem at the tip of the arrow.

Step 3: Identify the major causes of the problem. These will comprise the major "bones" of the diagram. These causes can be generated through brainstorming or they can be the different process stages.

Step 4: Draw and label the major "bones" as diagonal lines projecting off the backbone.

Step 5: Brainstorm for the reasons of these major causes by continually asking, "Why does this cause produce this effect?" Each time an answer is given, a small bone, representing the subcause, is drawn extending from the cause bone. Be sure to label this subcause. This is repeated until you have exhausted all possible answers.

Step 6: Identify the most likely root cause of the effect (problem) being studied and circle it.

Step 7: Verify that the most likely root cause has a significant impact on the effect. You can do this by collecting data on the metric that is associated with this root cause. You can then either use a line graph, trend line analysis, or scatter diagram that is discussed next in this section.

Special Notes
1. A CE diagram does not by itself identify the major root cause(s) of a problem.

2. Be sure to test the logic of the diagram, that is, make sure that every subcause is properly placed.

3. If one cause on the diagram appears to have many complicated subcauses, then construct a separate diagram for that cause.

4. Don't be afraid to make corrections or deletions.

5. The more a CE diagram is used, the more effective it becomes—so use it often.

6. CE diagrams are also used for positive investigations, such as benchmarking causes of exemplary performance.

Template for Cause-Effect Diagram

Category 1 Category 2 Category 3

Desired Effect

Category 4 Category 5

FIGURE 6.6. SAMPLE CAUSE-EFFECT DIAGRAM

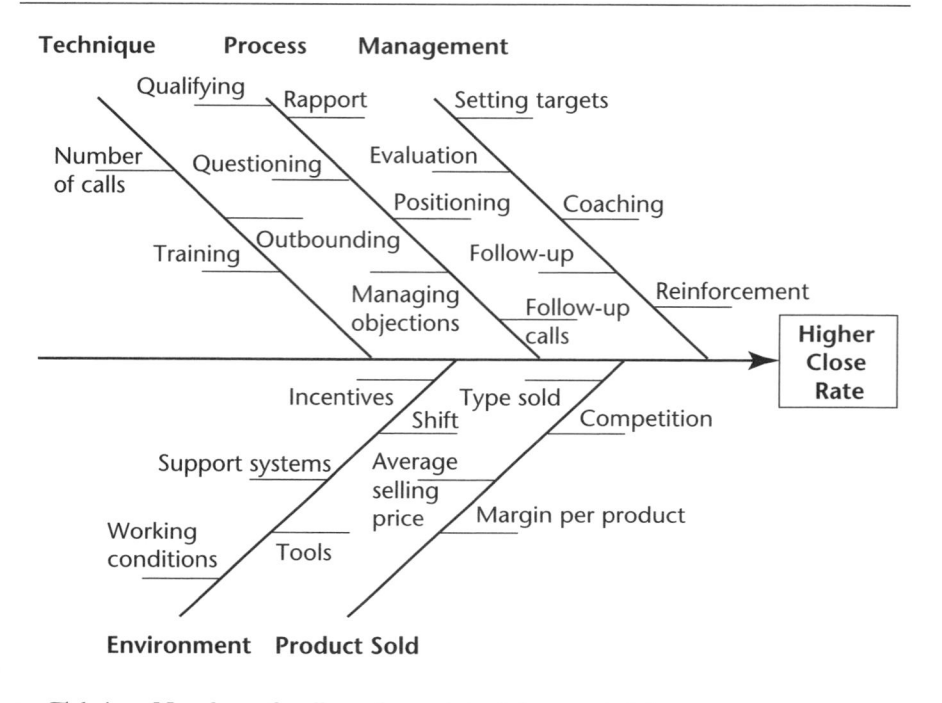

- *Technique.* Number of calls outbound, training, and style.
- *Process.* Qualifying customer needs, building rapport, positioning, questioning, managing objections, and conducting follow-up calls.
- *Product Being Sold.* Margin per product, average selling price, competition, and type.
- *Environment.* Working conditions, tools, support systems, shift, rewards, and incentives.
- *Management.* Setting targets and expectations, coaching, evaluating performance, follow-up, and reinforcement.

After listing all the subfactors under each major category in the diagram, the project team determined that the process category had the most impact on higher close rate. In a similar way, the focus group rated rewards and incentives highly as a key factor for improving performance. As a result, contests were held to motivate sales representatives to improve their close rates. The prizes for the winners every week included movie tickets, gift certificates, and cash. This yielded an average 5 percent increase in close rate for all the teams involved. Consequently, quota attainment, revenues, and profit margins also improved. In addition, close rate is now included in each sales representative's performance plan and is used as a major metric for recommending professional advancement and promotions for this business unit.

Scatter Diagrams. The last useful tool for analysis that will be covered in this chapter is the scatter diagram.

Five different scatter diagrams are displayed in Figure 6.7. Figure 6.7a shows that there is a strong positive relationship between x1 and y1 and indicates that an increase in y1 depends on increases in x1. Figure 6.7b shows that there is a positive relationship between x2 and y2; however, other factors seem to be influencing y2. Figure 6.7c shows there is no relationship between x3 and y3. Figure 6.7d shows a negative relationship between x4 and y4 and that other factors are affecting y4. Figure 6.7e shows a strong negative relationship between x5 and y5.

A scatter diagram by itself does not imply any statistical significance of the observed relationship. Additional analysis, such as correlation coefficients, has to be done. The implications drawn from a scatter diagram are only valid for the range of values that were actually plotted.

For example, in the consumer division of a high-tech company we worked with, we generated a scatter diagram to determine whether test results in a new hire class impacted sales revenue performance. We obtained test result data from new hire trainers and received weekly new hire revenue data from the sales operation team. We then generated a scatter diagram for three different tests versus sales revenues. The tests we used were product training, selling process, and services. Of the three, product training had the strongest relationship with sales revenues. The scatter diagram for this project looked like the one in Figure 6.7a, where there was a strong positive correlation between product training test results and sales revenues.

As a result of developing this scatter diagram, we recommended to the training manager that the product training portion of new hire class be looked at to ensure that it was effective and directly linked to specific performance objectives. An offshoot of this recommendation was a redesign of product training to make it hands-on, with plenty of skill applications, feedback, and practice. One particularly instructional strategy that was used for this module was creating a mini-fair with the actual products displayed in the room. Each new hire was asked specific questions when he or she visited each product station. The basic features, benefits to the customer, and competitive positioning strategy were included in the list of questions. It was extremely fun and effective and yielded improved performance.

Leveraging Results to Improve Performance

Once data are presented in meaningful formats, you can recommend specific actions for improving performance. Here are a few ways that you can leverage your measurement results to improve performance in your organization.

TOOL 15

CONSTRUCTING A SCATTER DIAGRAM

What It's About

A scatter diagram is a graph of point plots that is used to compare two variables. The distribution of the points indicates the cause-effect relationship (or lack thereof) between two variables. In order to use a scatter diagram, paired data must be available for the two variables being studied. For example, in a new hire sales training course we worked with in a computer sales organization, we studied the relationship between sales revenues and a product sales test. We found a strong relationship between test scores and sales revenue performance.

Purpose of Tool

Scatter diagrams are very useful in that they:

1. Can clearly indicate whether or not a cause-effect relationship exists between two variables, and

2. Give an idea of the strength of that relationship. For example, two variables may have a strong, moderate, weak, or no positive or negative relationship.

How to Customize

Step 1: Determine which two variables are to be paired and studied.

Step 2: Collect 50–100 paired samples of these variables and enter them on the data sheet. Make sure that you document who, what, when, where, and how the data were collected.

Step 3: Draw the x and y axes of the diagram. Typically the x axis is used for the controlled or "cause" variable, and the y axis is used for the predicted or "effect" variable.

Step 4: Plot the data. If data are repeated and fall on the same point, circle that point every time it is repeated.

Special Notes

1. Negative relationships are just as important as positive relationships.

2. The diagram does not guarantee that a relationship really exists. This is because the effect can be impacted by multiple factors. For example, if a plot of sales revenue vs. profit margin shows a strong relationship, it does not necessarily mean that sales revenue increased as a result of profit margin. There are other factors that can increase sales revenue, such as demand, marketing campaigns, and units sold.

3. The only conclusion that can be drawn from a scatter diagram is that x and y are related, but not that one causes the other.

4. Scatter diagrams are very useful and powerful, but they can easily be misused. Be sure you understand your data so you can make the right conclusions.

Template for a Scatter Diagram

Plot all paired observations here.

Variable Y

Variable X

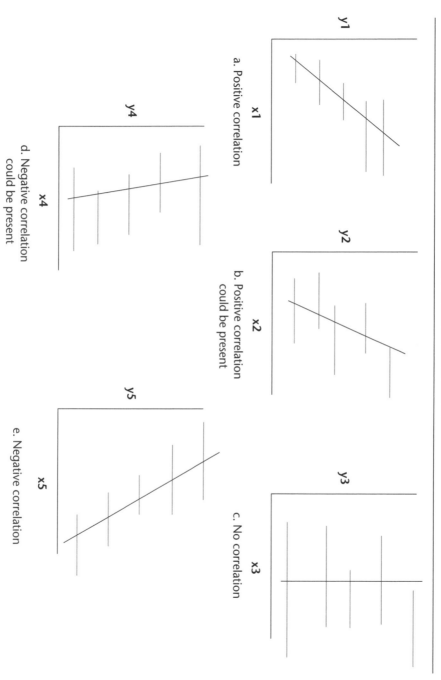

FIGURE 6.7. SAMPLE SCATTER DIAGRAMS

Coach Poor Performance

Based on measurement results, what evidence do you have that a particular employee needs coaching? First, analyze your line graph looking for downward trends. It is important that you compare current information with available baseline data. Baseline information is key, because if the downward trend is part of a cycle, then coaching is not needed. The "valleys" may be just part of fluctuations in the business cycle.

A trend line analysis can also help you identify coaching opportunities. If one of your employee's performance trend is downward, you can compute the rate at which performance decreases per period. You can then use this value to set performance targets.

In Figure 6.8 below, the high-end product revenue percentage is decreasing. This trend provides a coaching opportunity. A possible solution can be found by developing a cause-effect diagram to find out exactly what is causing this poor performance. Once the major cause for the problem is known, then appropriate steps can be taken.

It is important in sales situations that the sales manager consider the employee's performance on all measures and look at the overall picture. It is possible

FIGURE 6.8. REVENUE PERCENTAGE FOR SMALL ACCOUNTS GROUPS

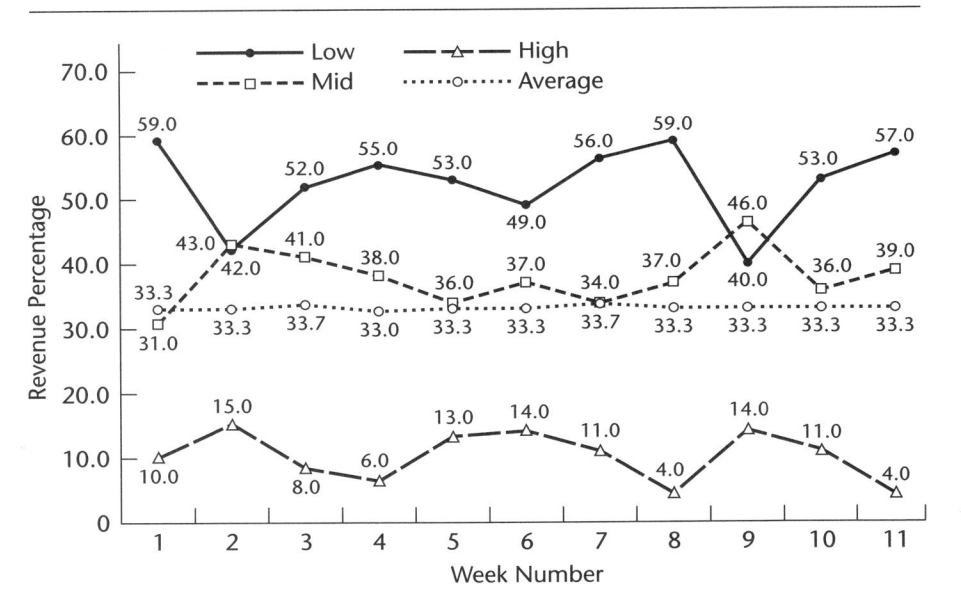

that performance is good in just one measure, at the expense of other equally important indicators, or performance may be poor on only one measure. A balanced analysis is required. For example, revenues can be very high, but if customer satisfaction is down, then something is wrong. A sales employee exceeding revenue expectations is not acceptable if average profit margin decreases as a result.

Reinforce and Benchmark Exemplary Performance

Reinforcement for good performance is rarely offered in the business world. It is very important to sustain improvement and motivate employees by reinforcing and rewarding good performers. In Figure 6.3, the line graph for the "big accounts" group clearly indicates an upward trend. In this situation, the manager should reinforce the performance of the big accounts group so that it is sustained. It is also worth doing a cause-effect diagram on the possible factors at work. These factors can then be shared with the rest of the sales employees so they can accomplish similar results.

Identify Possible Causes

As discussed earlier, you can use a cause-effect diagram to identify root causes of a performance problem. In the CE example on improving close rate, we saw that the major root cause of the problem was lack of appropriate incentives. Addressing a major root cause resulted in improved performance. It is possible that if the other root causes are addressed, the results would be even better. The point is that you can only expect performance improvement if the root cause or causes have been clearly identified.

In our experience with various companies and organizations, we have seen initiatives that failed during implementation because they addressed the symptoms, rather than the cause of the problem. Spending quality analysis time upfront can save rework and scrap later on. We have worked on projects that had to be redesigned, redefined, or scrapped halfway through the process because a cause analysis had not been done. For example, in a small printing company we consulted with, key executives asked for team-building training after managers complained that their employees did not relate well with one another. Team-building training was conducted for all employees, but executives noticed that the problem did not go away. Employees continued to work independently and were not open in communicating their concerns and issues with other "team" members. We were asked to determine why the team-building training had not worked. The first thing we did was develop a CE diagram to identify the sources of the problem. After talking with fifteen employees and three managers, we found out that the employees did not know that they were expected to share concerns and issues and communicate these to the managers. Thus, the problem was not knowledge and skills (that training can solve) but a problem of "communicating expectations." Instead of doing more team-building training, we talked with a focus group of managers to draft communication policies and expectations and put them on bulletin boards and posters around the company. Because of this, employees are now more open in sharing ideas and concerns with one another.

Determine Trends and Patterns

Trend line analysis and scatter diagrams can be used to determine patterns so that you can predict future performance. In the example shown in Figure 6.5, there is an increasing trend line on the number of low-end product units sold. The calculated increased rate of forty-two units per week can be used to project future weekly demand. These forecasts can help various functional areas in the business plan their resources, systems, and processes.

For example, human resources can plan on how many permanent and temporary employees they need to hire during specific periods; the marketing group can use these forecasts to determine the appropriate timing and aggressiveness of their campaigns. Manufacturing can use them to ensure that parts and supplies for production are available when needed; line managers can plan their employee schedules and time off based on these objective data.

A word of caution, though. Forecasting is not as simple as it sounds from our discussion here. There are multiple variables that impact sales revenue, productivity, and customer buying patterns. Complex forecasting models and detailed statistical analyses are done to deal with these variables in the real world, but measurement data does provide a strong backbone for helping a business accomplish its targets through accurate forecasting and performance projections.

◆ ◆ ◆

Key Summary Points

The following are the key points covered in this chapter.

1. Leveraging measurement results is as important as, if not more important than, collecting and presenting data. Its real value relies on how the data are used to improve performance.

2. When presenting data, consider factors such as the audience you want to reach, the purpose of your measurement, the data that are available, and the number of dimensions of data that you have collected.

3. One-dimensional presentation strategies are used to provide a "snapshot" view of performance, while two-dimensional or multi-dimensional strategies are used to present comparison, improvement, and change data.

4. The most common multi-dimensional strategies include line graphs, trend line analyses, cause-effect diagrams, and scatter diagrams.

5. Specific ways in which measurement data can be leveraged to improve performance include coaching poor performance, benchmarking exemplary performance, identifying root causes of performance problems, and projecting future performance.

APPLICATION EXERCISE: CASE STUDY, CHAPTER SIX

LEVERAGING RESULTS TO IMPROVE PERFORMANCE AT FJT TECH

Discussion: Questions and Answers

Using the knowledge you have gained in this chapter, here are some questions and their answers that will help you leverage the measurement results you generate to improve performance at FJT Tech.

1. Aside from the table framework that was discussed in Tool 10 in Chapter 5, what other strategies for presenting data will be valuable for FJT Tech?

    For tracking sales metrics of sales representatives and their sales teams, presenting them as a "snapshot-in-time" will not work. Sales revenues, profit margins, and market share percentages are very complex measures that are affected by multiple factors. Because of this complexity, you have to make room for data fluctuations and changes. Thus, you need to present these results as linear graphs or trend lines because trends and patterns are valuable in analyzing current performance. Performance may dip in one month due to factors beyond a sales employee's control, but if sales performance of a sales representative is improving in the long haul, then that presents the truer picture of performance. Therefore, present the data collected using the framework in Tool 13 as a line graph and not a table. You can also see how the employee is doing relative to the previous weeks by looking at the line graph. Figure 6.9 is an example of a line graph that shows product units sold for FJT Tech.

FIGURE 6.9. COMPARISON OF NUMBER OF UNITS SOLD

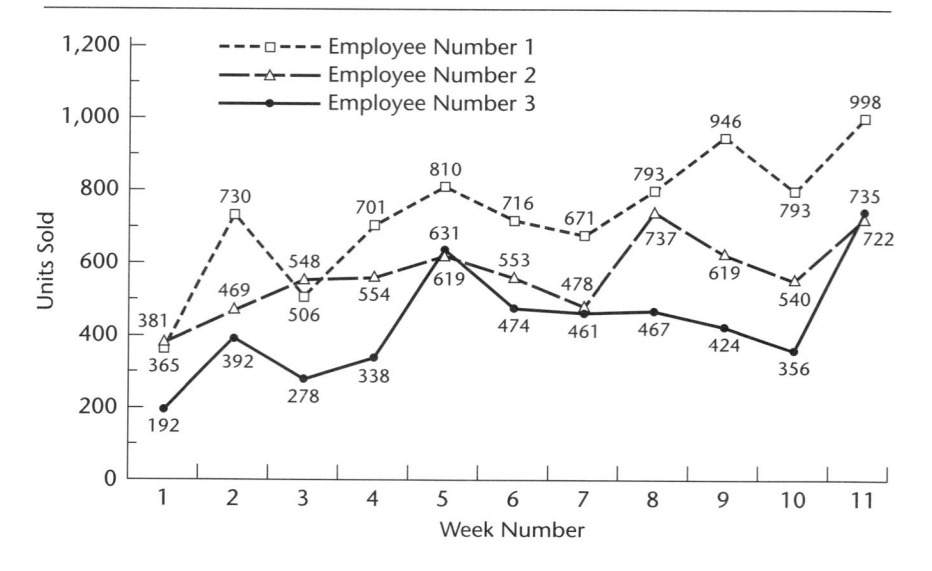

Also do a cause-effect analysis on determining the root causes of the performance gaps for FJT Tech, like the one in Figure 6.6 in Chapter Six. The cross-functional task force has identified a knowledge/skills gap in sales employees, so it will be worthwhile to identify what is causing this gap. The major categories in this cause-effect diagram can be the same categories that are listed in Figure 6.6. Figure 6.10 shows the cause-effect diagram that attempts to identify the causes of the skills gap.

FIGURE 6.10. CAUSE-EFFECT DIAGRAM
TO IMPROVE SELLING SKILLS

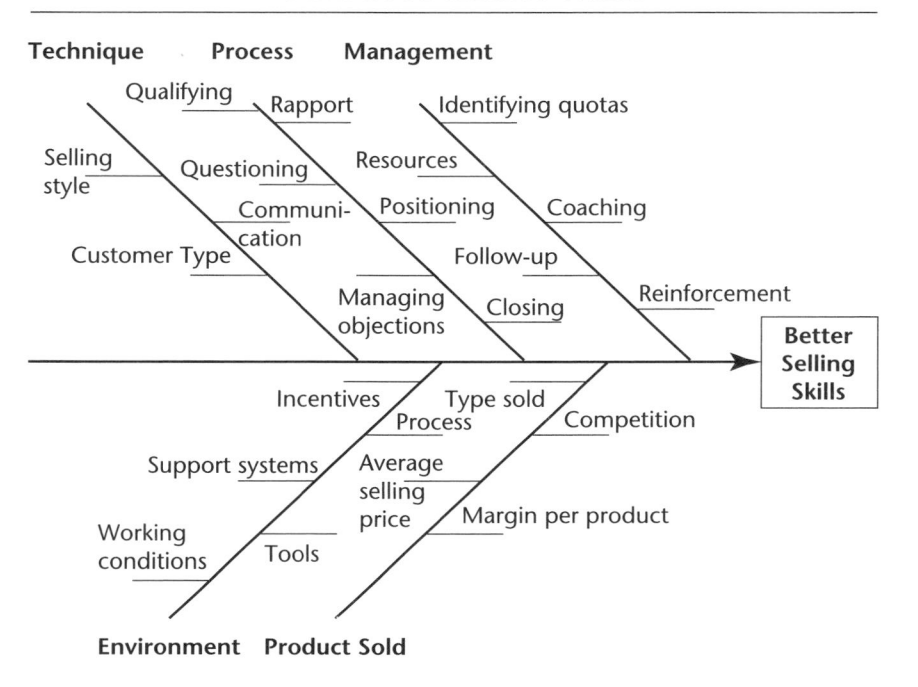

Another business solution that was selected by the cross-functional task force was to implement a massive advertising campaign when the new product is launched. It will be valuable to track whether this campaign is really responsible for the increase in sales of the new product when it is launched. A line graph that shows sales revenues each week (or daily if possible) will be helpful so that revenue performance can be compared when the specific advertising campaigns are implemented. The line graph for this will be similar to Figure 6.9. Finally, a scatter diagram can also be used to determine the key factors that contribute to improved sales performance. For FJT Tech, the variables that are appropriate in determining whether the strength of the relationship between them can be the following:

1. Number of advertisements rolled out vs. sales revenues for the week

2. Close rate vs. sales revenues

3. Customer satisfaction ratings vs. sales revenues

4. Customer satisfaction ratings vs. close rate

We are expecting positive relationships between the set of variables. We have experienced that advertisements, especially if they are targeted to the specific audience that they are trying to reach, have strong relationships with sales revenues. A good example is during the 1999 Super Bowl when a small Internet firm more than quintupled its sales because of the high-visibility, high-profile advertisement that was shown during half-time. For the organization, it was definitely worth spending huge amounts because the return on its investment showed on its bottom line.

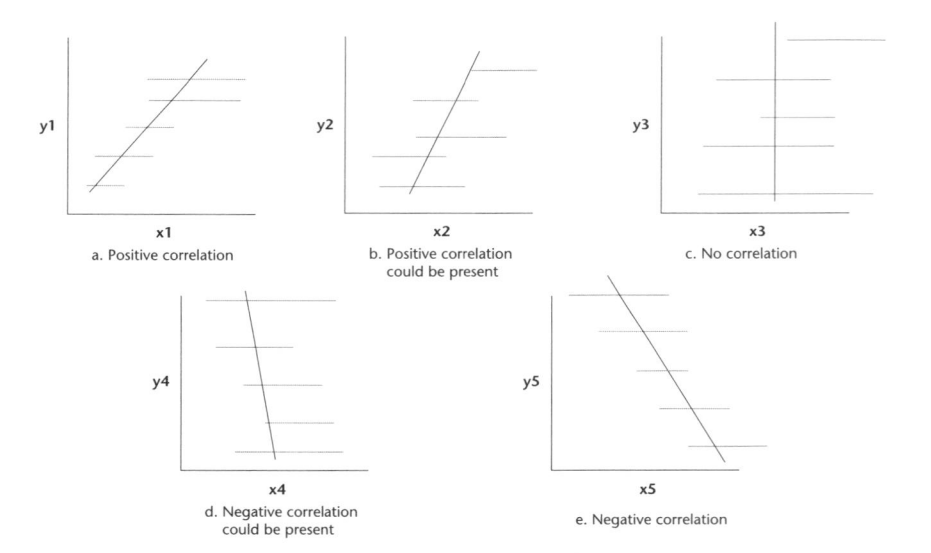

a. Positive correlation

b. Positive correlation could be present

c. No correlation

d. Negative correlation could be present

e. Negative correlation

If you plot variables 2 and 3, the resulting graph will be similar to b (Positive correlation) in the copy of Figure 6.7 from Chapter Six above, showing excellent performance by sales representatives. It is hard to find employees who have high close rates *and* sales revenues. For most people, they see that a sales representative had to sacrifice one for the other. We have found that you can improve your close rates and increase sales revenues at the same time. If sales representatives qualify their customers' needs up-front, they can close the sale better because they have information for positioning the close. Improving close rates does not always mean spending more time with the customer; it can also mean using the sales process correctly the first time.

2. How can you leverage the measurement results that you have generated to improve performance at FJT Tech?

   The same methods discussed in Chapter Six will apply directly to the FJT Tech situation. First, if revenue line graphs show a decreasing trend, that's a signal that a sales manager for a team or department has to coach constituents to reverse this trend. If the trend is increasing, the sales manager can benchmark good performance by interviewing top performers and asking them what they are doing differently that causes this improvement. Scatter diagram results on number of advertising campaigns versus sales revenues will be useful for conducting correlation studies on the relationship between the two variables. Once a correlation value is determined, marketing can then help forecast projected improvement in sales performance, given the number of advertisements that were rolled out during that time period.

RESOURCES

The resources listed in this section are divided into the stages of the performance measurement process that is introduced in the book. The sources in each stage are either referenced here or are suggested readings if you want to explore more about this stage.

Overview of Performance Measurement

Framework for the selection of performance measurement systems. [Homepage of Joint Commission on Accreditation of Healthcare Organizations], [Online]. (1997, October 3–last update). Available: http://www.jcaho.org/perfmeas/oryx/critinfo.html [1998, July 21].

Hale, J. (1998). *The performance consultant's fieldbook.* San Francisco: Jossey-Bass/Pfeiffer.

How to measure performance: A handbook of techniques and tools, [Online]. Available: http://www.llnl.gov/PBM/handbook/p25.html [1998, July 7].

Kirkpatrick, D. (1967). Evaluation of training. In R. Craig & L. Bittles (Eds.), *Training and Development Handbook.* New York: McGraw-Hill.

Organizational-level performance measurement for external benchmarking. [Homepage of KSC Research and Technology], [Online]. (1996, May 22–last update). Available: http://technology.ksc.nasa.gov/WWWaccess/95report/ief/ie14.html [1998, July 21].

Performance measurement. [Homepage of B. L. Seamon & Associates, Inc.], [Online]. (1997, May 10–last update). Available: http://www.blseamon.com/perform.html [1998, July 26].

Performance measurement. [Homepage of Organization for Economic Cooperation and Development], [Online]. (1997, August 5–last update). Available: http://www.oecd.org/puma/mgmtres/pac/perform.html [1998, July 26].

Performance measurement. [Homepage of Organizational Solutions Group], [Online]. (1997, September 3–last update). Available: http://www.erols.com/os-group/PerfMeas.html [1998, July 21].

Phillips, J.J. (1994). *Measuring return on investment.* Washington, DC: American Society for Training and Development.

Process measurement. [EDGE Software, Inc.], [Online]. (1997, 1998–copyright date). Available: http://search.excite.com/search.gw?c=web&s=performance+measurement [1998, July 21].

Strategic planning. [Homepage of Organizational Solutions Group], [Online]. (1997, September 3–last update). Available: http://www.erols.com/os-group/StratPlng.html [1998, July 21].

Training Impact Group. (1998). *Designing training to achieve business results.* Performance Measurements for Training Conference, Orlando, FL.

Worthen, B., & Sanders, J. (1987). *Educational evaluation: Alternative approaches and practical guidelines.* New York: Longman.

Establishing the Business Case

Conner, D.R. (1993). *Managing at the speed of change.* New York: Villard.

O'Brien, Y. (1995). Cost-benefit analysis worksheet. Austin, TX. Unpublished document.

Robinson, D.G., & Robinson, J.C. (1995). *Performance consulting: Moving beyond training.* San Francisco: Berrett-Koehler.

Identifying the Right Performance Metrics

American Productivity and Quality Center (APQC) International Benchmarking Clearinghouse. (1997). *Metrics management guide.* Houston, TX: Author.

Implementing the Performance Measurement System

Brown, M. G. (1996). *Keeping score: Using the right metrics to drive world-class performance.* New York: Quality Resources.

Kaydos, W. (1991). *Measuring, managing, and maximizing performance.* Cambridge, MA: Productivity Press.

Lynch, R.I., & Cross, K.F. (1991). *Measure up! Yardsticks for continuous improvement.* Cambridge, MA: Blackwell.

Maskell, B.H. (1994). *New performance measures.* Portland, OR: Productivity Press.

Thor, C.G. (1994). *The measures of success: Creating a high performance organization.* Essex Junction, VT: Omneo, Oliver Wright Publications.

Leveraging Results to Improve Performance

Brassard, M. (1989). *The memory jogger: Featuring the seven management and planning tools.* Methuen, MA: GOAL/QPC.

Juran, J. (1989). *Juran on leadership for quality* (4th ed.). New York: McGraw-Hill.

Swift, J.A. (1995). *Introduction to modern statistical quality control and management.* Delray Beach, FL: St. Lucie Press.

INDEX

CD-ROM INSTRUCTIONS

SYSTEM REQUIREMENTS

Windows PC

- 386, 486, or Pentium processor-based personal computer
- Microsoft Windows 3.1, Windows 95, or Windows NT 3.51 or later
- Minimum RAM: 4 MB for Windows 3.1, 8 MB for Windows 95 and NT
- Available space on hard disk: 4 MB Windows 3.1, 8 MB Windows 95 and NT
- 2X speed CD-ROM drive or faster
- Netscape 3.0 or higher browser or MS Internet Explorer 3.0 or higher

YEAR 2000 COMPLIANCE

The *Implementing Global Performance Measurement Systems* CD-ROM is "Year 2000 Compliant," by which we mean that this CD-ROM will not (i) experience any abnormality, malfunction, breakdown, degradation, or impairment of any kind in calculating, comparing, sequencing, or otherwise processing data or information simply as a result of, or related in any way to, the passage of time or changing date values (including without limitation dates from, into, and during the 20th and 21st centuries, including any leap years); or (ii) cause any of the foregoing problems in interfacing with your Company's systems.

GETTING STARTED

1. Insert the CD-ROM into your drive.
2. Close the drive.
3. In a few moments, the CD-ROM should start automatically.

Your default web browser will come up on your desktop with the *Global Performance Measurement Systems* curriculum.

MOVING AROUND

The flowchart in the center of the main screen illustrates the sequence of the performance measurement process. You can click on any of the boxes in the flowchart for a list of deliverables to complete each process step. To return to the main screen at any time, simply click on "*Global Performance Measurement Systems*" in the top left corner of the screen.

You can use the navigational toolbar on the upper left-hand side of the main screen to jump between major sections of the CD-ROM. By clicking on the buttons in the toolbar you can get to the sections described below.

Process. This section describes the overall process for implementing a global performance measurement system, including the steps, system criteria, and techniques for positioning performance measurement in your organization. This provides the framework for the deliverables and downloadable tools that are included in the next sections.

Deliverables. This section contains the list of deliverables for each step that is outlined in the performance measurement process described in the Process section. Templates are then developed for each of these deliverables so you can use them for your organization. Each deliverable contains a description (What It Is About), uses and applications (Purpose), tips for modifying for your organization (How To Customize), and sample application (Example).

Download. This section allows you to download blank templates for each of the tools listed in the Deliverables section. These templates are in Microsoft Word, Excel, or PowerPoint format.

Case Study. To ensure application of theories and tools presented in the Process and Deliverables sections, a comprehensive case study on implementing a global performance measurement system for FJT Tech is presented in this section. The case study showcases concrete examples on how the steps in the cookbook process are followed. It also exemplifies how each tool was used to complete the required deliverables in each step of the measurement approach.

Certain sections such as the Deliverables section have a secondary navigation system represented in the white links. These links can be used to view subsections within the sections.

IN CASE OF TROUBLE

If you experience difficulty using the *Implementing Global Performance Measurement Systems* CD-ROM, please follow these steps:
1. Make sure your hardware and systems configurations conform to the systems requirements noted under "Systems Requirements" on p. 152.
2. Review the installation procedure for your type of hardware and operating system. It is possible to reinstall the software if necessary.
3. You may call Jossey-Bass Customer Service at (415) 433-1740 between the hours of 8 A.M. and 5 P.M. Pacific Time, and ask for Jossey-Bass CD-ROM Technical Support, or e-mail the author, Ferdinand Tesoro, at Ferdinand_Tesoro@Dell.com.
   Before calling, please have the following information available:

- Type of computer and operating system
- Version of Windows being used
- Any error messages displayed
- Complete description of the problem

(It is best if you are sitting at your computer when making the call.)